D1084273

Ulrich Krause

NLB

Money and Abstract Labour

On the Analytical Foundations of Political Economy

Translated by Pete Burgess

Edited by Jon Rothschild

British Library
Cataloguing in Publication Data

Krause, Ulrich
 Money and abstract labour.
 1. Marxian economics
 I. Title   II. Geld und abstrakte Arbeit.
 English
 335.4'08   HB97.5

 ISBN 0-86091-049-0
 ISBN 0-86091-749-5 Pbk

082812

First published as Geld und abstrakte Arbeit
by Campus Verlag, Frankfurt
© Campus Verlag GmbH, 1979

This edition first published 1982
© NLB, 1982
NLB and Verso Editions, 15 Greek Street, London W1

'Preface to the English Edition'
translated by John Hampson

Typeset in Compugraphic Century Schoolbook by
Red Lion Setters, London WC1N 2LA

Printed and bound by
Redwood Burn Ltd,
Trowbridge, Wiltshire

Contents

Preface to the English Edition

It is simply no longer possible to ignore the fact that contemporary economic analyses deal extensively with quantitative problems, to which mathematical techniques are applied. This is true of analyses of various persuasions, Marxist in particular. The past decade has seen the publication of a gamut of excellent monographs making use of mathematics to examine quantitative problems in the framework of Marxist theory. This procedure is relatively straightforward so long as it concerns physical measurements, but it can become dubious if applied, as though it were unproblematic, to variables whose economic significance itself has yet to be established with sufficient precision. Mathematical methods can then simulate a precision that is actually lacking. The recent monographs, for example, present many interesting quantitative conclusions about prices and labour-values even though they do not delve into the qualitative concepts integral to an understanding of prices and values, namely money and abstract labour.

As far as I know, the mathematically oriented analyses of Marxist economics—and not only the more recent ones—do not examine money and abstract labour any more closely. This can be seen in the continuing strife, now a century old, over the so-called transformation from (labour) values to (money) prices: the clashes have often been ringing, but the arena dimly lit. The treatment of money and abstract labour has so far been restricted to more qualitatively and verbally pitched investigations, following the example of Marx. Moreover, the really penetrating insights have been contributed much less by traditional Marxists than by a few more philosophically oriented revisionists. In particular, these authors revivified a subject that had withered to near extinction in orthodox Marxism: analysis of the value-form. Their aim, in accordance with the intentions of Marx himself, was to analyse money and abstract labour.

Unfortunately, the existing works on this question are neither especially clear nor at all rigorous. It must also be admitted that analysis of the value-form is among the favourite refuges of the 'obscurantism' so convincingly skewered by Ian Steedman. My intention in this book is to offer as clear and rigorous as possible an examination of 'Marx's triangle' and its vertices: money, abstract labour, and the value-form.

My hope is on the one hand to open the quantitatively oriented analyses to the themes of value-form, money, and abstract labour, and on the other to complement the qualitative treatment of these themes with analytic arguments. In my view it is not important whether the reflections presented here are in line with Marx or Marxism. Nevertheless, in much I do hold to the ideas of Marx, who was the first, as far as I know, to fruitfully analyse the terrain described by the above-mentioned triangle. Moreover, I see Marx's reflections as an approximate, albeit imposing, outline rather than an exposition based on clear and rigorous concepts; his discussion of abstract labour in particular, I would argue, is criss-crossed by thoroughly distinct notions.

The Content of the Book

Chapter 1 develops a stylized basic model, the various components of which are dealt with in later chapters. I first consider commodities, the production of which requires labour; since there are numerous commodities, numerous types of labour will have to be taken into account. Only types of labour specific to particular commodities will be considered, but this is not a fundamental limitation. Chapter 2 deals with the value-form, or more precisely, the value relation, a relation between any two quantities of commodities that depicts the direct and indirect exchange of these commodities and exhibits the corresponding properties of the exchange.

It is perhaps not inappropriate to emphasize that the concept of the value-form is here defined without reference to labour, and still less to labour-'value'. (In the literature labour 'values' often somehow fall ready-made from heaven, which makes analysis of the value-form superfluous or reduces it to an exercise in Marxist duty.) My analysis of the value-form goes back to Marx, who endorsed, albeit somewhat half-heartedly, S. Bailey's objections to Ricardo's notion of an invariant measure and absolute value. For Marx, analysis of the form of value was the key to investigation of both money and abstract labour (see chapter 2, note 1).

Discussion of the value-form leads to what I call the transitivity problem: how do the many mutually independent acts of exchange yield an exchange equilibrium that can be described by a price vector. Some reflections about this problem go all the way back to Cournot, and later Walras. Their notions, which have been picked up again more recently, seek an answer in the value-form/money side of Marx's triangle (see chapter 2, note 4, and chapter 3, notes 2 and 6).

The special role of money (-commodities) in the framework of the value relation is the theme of chapter 3. Money is shown to be significant not only as a quantity, but also, because of the interlacing of indirect exchange, as a special structure. The circularity of the transaction-structure, which mirrors exchange relations, is discussed, as an analogue to Sraffa's approach to the production-structure. The structural aspect of money is also relevant to the so-called quantity-equation of money. We will examine how the sum of money required to effect all transactions depends both on the transaction-structure and on the localization of this sum of money. The role of money as a store of value and related questions will not be examined.

From chapter 4 onwards, the role of labour will be examined more closely. The aim of the exposition is not to erect a labour theory of value but to investigate labour itself, and in particular the implications for labour of the fact that the products of labour stand in a value relation to one another. Chapter 4 is concerned primarily with concrete—and heterogeneous—labour and demonstrates that, from a macro-economic standpoint, a complex of expenditures of the most diverse types of labour lies behind every unit of commodities.

In chapter 5 it is shown that the value-form—or better, the money relation—of the products of labour induces an 'equating' (in given quantities, called reduction co-efficients) of the various concrete labours. More specifically, this 'equating', provided it satisfies two simple requirements, is an equivalence relation on the set of the various concrete labours. Concrete labour viewed in terms of this equivalence relation is designated abstract labour.

An initial consequence of this concept of abstract labour is that all money commodities induce the same money relation, which resolves the transitivity problem. A second consequence is that relative prices and expenditures of labour, measured in abstract labour, coincide quantitatively. This fundamental relation reveals a close link between the spheres of circulation and production. It must, however, be noted that the magnitude of the relative expenditures of labour as abstract labour remains undetermined, since the reduction-coefficients are undetermined. Although the fundamental relation affords no quantitative determination of relative prices, it does describe, in the form of the exchange curve, the possible latitude of relative prices.

Chapter 6 describes the production of commodities, now through the concept of abstract labour. In particular, a macro-economic distribution relation is derived, in the form of the reproduction curve.

To quantitatively determine the relative expenditures of labour in terms of abstract labour and thereby relative prices, a quantitative determination of the relative reduction co-efficients is required. Both classical labour theory of value and its contemporary versions are distinguished by their assumption, as far as abstract labour is concerned, that the reduction-coefficients are all equal to 1. This assumption, as arbitrary as it is venerable, is criticized here as the dogma of homogeneous labour. In Adam Smith's famous example of the exchange of deer and beaver, the quantitative determination of the exchange ratio through labour-value is forced by implicitly assuming a reduction-coefficient of 1. In this book, in contrast, it is argued that consideration of labour-value in this example leads not to a quantitatively determined exchange ratio, but only to an exchange curve, which in this case actually leaves the exchange ratio completely open. (Viewed from this perspective, the example does not achieve what it was once supposed to).

Finally, chapter 7 undertakes a quantitative determination of the relative reduction-coefficients through the 'standard reduction of labour'. The term should suggest that what is involved is a dual counterpart to Sraffa's standard commodity; the standard reduction is to the various concrete labours as the standard commodity is to the various concrete commodities. Although the economic relevance of the standard reduction may be debatable, it has two interesting consequences. First, it reduces the multi-sectoral interconnection of many variables to a single macro-economic distribution relationship between the wage level, divided by the price level, and the rate of profit. Second, it casts new light on the classic transformation and reduction problems, such that the one proves to be the twin of the other.

Each chapter of the book (except the first) opens with a simple formulation of the basic question dealt with in that chapter; at the close of each chapter (except the last) the core of the answer to that chapter's basic question is summarized. Notes to each chapter are at the end of the book; they provide references, sometimes in great detail, to the literature in the field and its relationship to the present work. (Full bibliographic details are given the first time a work is cited; thereafter only the name of the author and an abbreviated title are given).

The mathematical appendix collects the mathematical techniques used in the book. Propositions that may be found in the literature are given without proof; references, of course, are listed. Those few propositions for which proofs are not contained in any of the works cited are given with proofs.

Additional Bibliography

I would like to take the opportunity presented by publication of this English edition to mention several works with which I became familiar only after the German edition appeared. These are listed in the additional bibliography and will be cited here by author and year of publication.

In my view, the dichotomy referred to at the beginning of this introduction persists. On the one hand, we find systematic, analytic investigations that do not concern themselves with the themes represented in 'Marx's triangle'. On the other hand, we find more philosophical analyses, linked to Marx's analysis of the value-form, which, however, fail to comprehend their object with sufficient clarity and rigour.

I would like to draw attention to one development in particular: the rising attention that has recently been paid to the heterogeneity of labour. The consideration of heterogeneous labour—which is fundamentally required given the production of a multiplicity of commodities—entails serious difficulties for both Marxist and neo-Ricardian theories. Indeed, a number of authors hold that the heterogeneity of labour poses a much more serious problem than the heterogeneity of capital, fruitfully analysed in the Cambridge (UK) versus Cambridge (US) debate. Several authors have tried to extend the 'fundamental Marxian theorem' to heterogeneous labour. 'The Marxian Theory of Value and Heterogeneous Labour: a Critique and Reformulation', the seminal essay by Bowles and Gintis published in 1978, has had great resonance. (See Morishima 1978; Holländer 1978; Reich 1979; Catephores 1981; McKenna 1981; and the responses of Bowles and Gintis: 1978, 1981a, and 1981b).

A 'fundamental Marxian theory' for heterogeneous labour can also be derived by means of the standard reduction of labour presented in this book. See Krause 1981a. The definition of the standard reduction given there, independent of the fundamental relationship, is equivalent to that given here. See also the discussion of exploitation as a 'system-wide phenomenon' in Steedman 1981). Whereas the articles referred to above are based on a Sraffa-style multi-sectoral model without joint production, Fujimori also deals with heterogeneous labour including joint production, in the framework of a von Neumann model. (Fujimori 1978; see also Krause 1981b and the revised version in Fujimori 1981).

Finally, I would also like to mention that many of the propositions of the present work, especially those on abstract labour and the standard reduction, also hold, in modified form, under joint production (Krause 1979).

Acknowledgements

I would like to thank students, colleagues, and friends for the many useful suggestions I have received from them, from an initial discussion paper of 1977, 'Form des Werts, abstrakte Arbeit und Preis', to the publication of this English edition. I am especially grateful to K. Gerlach and K.H. Hennings for the German edition of this work (1979), and to H.D. Kurz, M. Krüger, B. Rowthorn, and I. Steedman for this English edition. Although I am thankful to these and others for the elimination of errors, I have only myself to thank for the errors that remain.

This edition corresponds to the German edition with the exception of the new introduction and the additional bibliography.

Bremen, January 1982

1
The Basic Model and the Commodity Form

The wealth of modern market-societies consists to a very great extent of material goods that differ both in their utility for human beings and in their values; in other words, commodities.[1]

This is not necessary conceptually, nor has it always been so. To explore the commodity-form of present-day wealth, a few elementary distinctions are required, which also correspond to real differences that have arisen historically (although this aspect is not dealt with here; a number of interesting points can be found in the relevant anthropological and ethnological literature).[2]

Wealth is the result of a specific association (a metabolism) between human beings and nature. It is therefore necessary first of all to distinguish the human from the other, non-human part of nature. Figure 1 represents the situation diagrammatically.

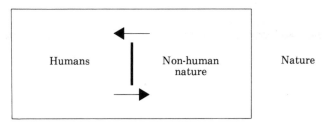

Figure 1

From the standpoint of the maintenance of the human species, this unity within nature means that the physical basis of humanity as a species lies in nature, including natural

processes, while the species masters parts of nature to secure
its survival, as shown symbolically in fig. 2.

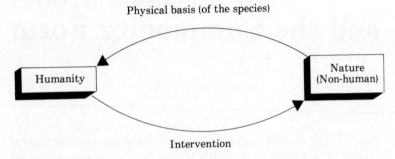

Figure 2

Subsequent distinctions will simply assume that nature
underlies the long-term physical basis of the human species and
will concentrate exclusively on differentiating human interven-
tion in nature. This consists essentially of the human appropriation of nature through labour (for example, fish have to be
found, caught, and prepared). This active appropriation serves
in turn to sustain the capacity of the individual to work, as
depicted symbolically in fig. 3.

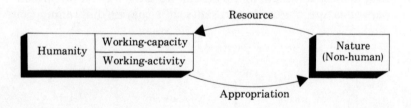

Figure 3

Just as working-capacity can be differentiated (between
young and old, for example), so also can activity be divided
according to the part of nature appropriated (hunting and fish-
ing, for example). Both types of distinction yield a division of

labour (gender-specific in its earliest forms). From the standpoint of labour, a central new distinction within humanity's association with nature thus emerges. Nature serves as a resource for labour, supplying raw-materials; but the appropriation of nature is accomplished with the aid of products of human labour. The decisive point is this: the products of human labour, the results of this labour, thus become natural prerequisites for further labour. This role of the products of labour as a 'second nature' lends great significance to the relationship of humanity to itself—although this is an ever-present relationship—alongside the relation between humanity and nature. At this stage it becomes meaningful to refer to social or economic structure. The essential moments of the *economic structure* can be listed succinctly.

1. Production: the manufacture of products using products and labour, with nature as the resource.

2. Distribution: the recycling of products as prerequisites of production, as means of production on the one hand (in accordance with the organization, or division, of labour) and as means of consumption on the other.

3. Consumption: the use of natural objects and products of human labour in order, among other things, to sustain the various sorts of working-capacity.

The interconnection of these three moments of the overall structure is illustrated in figure 4.

The essential new element is the feedback through *distribution*, which necessarily raises the issue of social or economic structure.[3] As the direct interaction with nature is severed, the economic structure emerges as the new kernel of the metabolism. In investigating this structure more closely, in particular the role of labour and the distribution feedback, we will regard it as a result of the metabolism between humanity and nature, although there will be no further explicit consideration of its relationship to non-human nature. Raw-materials as prerequisites of production are treated only inasmuch as they are

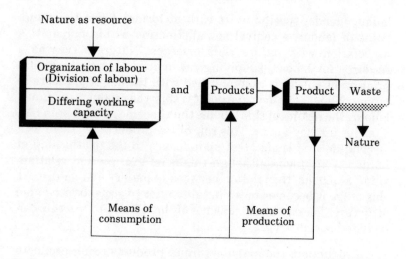

Distribution

Figure 4

products of labour, and likewise the means of consumption required to sustain the capacity to work. Those products of labour that do not assume useful forms—waste, in the broadest sense—will not be considered (pollution, for example).

In this study, production, distribution, and their mutual relationship will be viewed chiefly in terms of the feedback described above. Consumption is therefore of interest only as a moment of distribution. Its relationship to labour, to the maintenance of working-capacity, will be left open for the present. The individual moments are then as follows.

Production (P):   Labour (of different types) plus
products yields products   (1)

Distribution (D):   Products $\nearrow$ Means of production
$\searrow$ Means of consumption   (2)

In this dual representation of production and distribution, the connection between the two is expressed through the feedback mechanism, as shown in figure 5, which clarifies the feedback and leaves the relationship between consumption and labour open for subsequent analysis.

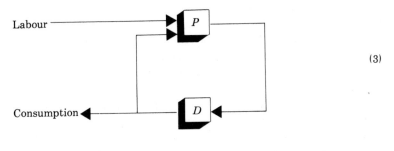

(3)

Figure 5

The basic economic model formulated in (1), (2), and (3), with the moments of production, distribution, and consumption, economically characterizes the specific form of society to which it corresponds.

As (3) shows, the character of the economic structure is highly dependent on the nature of distribution. Many systems are conceivable, and many have arisen historically. That labour, of different types, is necessary for their preservation is true of all societies. What differs is *how* these various labours are related and coordinated, and that depends on the specific mode of distribution (see chapter 6).

Historical forms of distribution have rested on such highly diverse and generally complex relationships as kinship, rites of sacrifice, systems of gift and tribute, forms of limited exchange of products, and combinations of all these, although one may often have predominated.[4]

The principle of distribution in a market society is based on private property in the means of production, and the mediation of the output of private production through the market. The relationship between products and people rests on the fact that the means of production are at the disposal of independent and autonomous individuals and are not controlled through communal or kinship relations. The specific social structure implied by this—a society of free and equal individuals, the *'juridical form'*—will not be considered here as such.[5] The products of labour are exchanged for one another on the market, become inputs for additional production. Products therefore have not only a use-value for individuals, but also a particular exchange-value among themselves. Inasmuch as they possess both, the products of human labour may be called commodities. When the products of labour assume the *commodity-form*, the connection between human beings and their products comes to rest on two distinct spheres, that of individuals, mediated through law, and that of commodities, mediated through value. The relation between the two spheres is that the individuals are owners of commodities, the commodities the property of individuals. Although investigation of a market economy will follow later, here it is appropriate to note the basic distinction between market societies and other types of society, from the standpoint of the mode of distribution (see fig. 6).

Market principle	Persons	Products
Persons	Form of law (for individuals)	Private owner
Products	Private property	Value-form (for commodities)

Figure 6

The basic model for the analysis that follows consists of the economic structure formulated in (1), (2), and (3), with distribution in the specific form of products as commodities, and production in the specific form of private property in the means of production. This basic model can be represented in greater detail if it is kept in mind that commodities appear as certain quantities of a particular unit (litre, tonne, bushel, etc.) and that labours of different types occupy a certain span of time, once a suitable unit is selected (hours, for example).

Let, therefore, $\{C_1, \ldots, C_n\}$ represent a collection of commodities of any arbitrary but fixed units. In order to produce commodity C_i, a specific labour, which we will call labour of type i, is required. For example, to produce the commodity 'linen', labour of the type 'weaving' is required. The duration of labour can be measured in any desired unit of time, but it, like the unit for the commodity itself, must be retained throughout. If t_{ji} is the number of units of commodity C_j required as means of production to produce y_i units of commodity C_i, and x_i is the amount of labour of type i so required, then relation (1) can be represented as follows.

$(x_i$ of type $i, t_{1i}C_1, t_{2i}C_2, \ldots, t_{ni}C_n) \to y_i C_i$ for $i = 1, 2, \ldots, n$

or briefly,

$(x_i, t_{1i}, t_{2i}, \ldots, t_{ni}) \to y_i$ for $i = 1, 2, \ldots, n$.

The numbers x_i, y_i, and t_{ji} are non-negative. For certain i and j, $t_{ji} = 0$, namely when commodity C_j is not (directly) required to produce commodity C_i. In contrast, $y_i > 0$ for every i, and since only products of labour are being counted, $x_i > 0$ for every i as well. Productivity is expressed in the ratios $\frac{t_{ji}}{y_i}$ and $\frac{x_i}{y_i}$.

For any given level of productivity, expressed in the ratios $a_{ji} = \frac{t_{ji}}{y_i}$, $l_i = \frac{x_i}{y_i}$, production can be more precisely formulated as follows:

$$(l_i, a_{1i}, a_{2i}, \ldots, a_{ni}) \to 1, \qquad i = 1, 2, \ldots, n. \tag{1'}$$

In words, the production of one unit of product C_i requires a_{1i} units of C_1, a_{2i} units of product C_2, etc., and l_i units of labour of type i. If diag l denotes the $n \times n$ diagonal matrix containing the elements l_i in the diagonal, A the $n \times n$ matrix of the coefficients a_{ij}, and I the $n \times n$ identity matrix, then (1') can be expressed more concisely in matrix form as:

$$(\text{diag } l, A) \to I$$

which should be read in columns. (See the mathematical appendix for explanations of vectors and matrices). If it is assumed that the production of a given multiple of commodity C_i requires corresponding multiples of commodities C_1 to C_n and of labour, then the relations expressing the production of y_i units of C_i are:

$$(l_i y_i, a_{1i} y_i, a_{2i} y_i, \ldots, a_{ni} y_i) \rightarrow y_i \text{ for } i = 1, \ldots, n.$$

Or, in matrix form, with $y = (y_1, y_2, \ldots, y_n)$

$$(\text{diag } l \cdot \text{diag } y, A \cdot \text{diag } y) \rightarrow \text{diag } y \qquad (1'')$$

also to be read in columns.

Let us now assume that a vector y of quantities of the products is manufactured in accordance with this relationship. Since the means of production are privately owned, the quantities of products y_i will be held by the various individual commodity owners. Before production can continue, these quantities must be distributed, each owner's amount being exchanged for certain amounts belonging to other owners.

Let y_{ij} be the quantity of C_i acquired by the owner of commodity C_j, where $i \neq j$. Then y_{jj} represents the amount of C_j that the owner of C_j does not exchange (strictly speaking, that he exchanges with himself). For $i, j = 1, 2, \ldots, n$, $y_{ij} \geq 0$; (y_{ij} can be zero, if the owner of C_j does not acquire any of C_i, because it fulfils no consumption or production need). Since the owner of commodity C_i owns exactly y_i units of C_i, and since this quantity is exchanged in portions or is not exchanged at all, $y_i = \sum_{j=1}^{n} y_{ij}$ for $i = 1, 2, \ldots, n$.

If Y denotes the $n \times n$ matrix of the y_{ij}, then aggregate exchange E consists in the association of a matrix Y with a produced vector y:

$$E: y \rightarrow Y \text{ where } y_i = \sum_{j=1}^{n} y_{ij}.$$

Distribution also has to do with how each commodity owner divides the quantity y_{ij} of commodity C_i into means of consumption and means of production. In other words, $y_{ij} = k_{ij} + \bar{y}_{ij}$, where k_{ij} denotes the quantity of means of consumption and $\bar{y}_{ij}$ the quantity of means of production. If K denotes the $n \times n$

matrix of the k_{ij}, and $\overline{Y}$ the $n \times n$ matrix of the $\overline{y}_{ij}$, then distribution is given by the transition from y to Y, and partition by $Y = K + \overline{Y}$. To specify (2), then, for distribution based on exchange, we have

$$y_i \to (y_{i1}, y_{i2}, \ldots y_{in}), \text{ where } y_i = \sum_{j=1}^{n} y_{ij} \text{ and } y_{ij} = k_{ij} + \overline{y}_{ij}$$
for $i, j = 1, 2, \ldots, n$. $\qquad\qquad$ (2′)

Or,

$$E\colon y \to Y, \text{ where } y = Yu, \ Y = K + \overline{Y} \qquad (2'')$$

in which $u = (1, 1, \ldots, 1)$, the n-vector whose components are all 1.

If production is continued on the basis of this distribution, and if we let $\overline{y} = (\overline{y}_1, \overline{y}_2, \ldots, \overline{y}_n)$ be the vector of the quantities of output produced, then for all i and j it must be the case that $\overline{y}_{ij} = a_{ij} \cdot \overline{y}_j$. In matrix form, $\overline{Y} = A \cdot \text{diag } \overline{y}$. The amount of labour required to produce $\overline{y}$ is given by $\text{diag } l \cdot \text{diag } \overline{y}$.

On the basis of the specifications (1″) and (2″), the interrelation of production and distribution expressed in (3) can be represented by fig. 7, wherein, proceeding on the basis of $y\colon$ $Y = E(y)$, $\overline{Y} = A \cdot \text{diag } \overline{y}$, $K = Y - \overline{Y}$, $\overline{L} = \text{diag } l \cdot \text{diag } \overline{y}$.

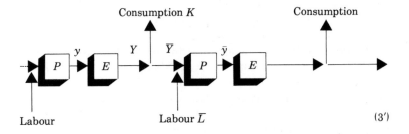

Figure 7

If $\overline{y} = y$, then (3′) reduces to a closed system, as depicted in (3). In general, however, (3′) consists of a succession of such models.[6] The step that generates (3′), namely the transition from y to $\overline{y}$, is as follows.

$$P: (\text{diag } l \cdot \text{diag } \bar{y}, \, E(y) - K) \rightarrow \text{diag } \bar{y} \qquad (3'')$$

Disregarding the division of commodities among the individual owners, and considering only the amounts relating to the sum total of owners, it follows that if we sum the columns of $Y = K + A \cdot \text{diag } \bar{y}$ we have

$$y = k + A\bar{y}$$

where $k_i = \sum\limits_{j=1}^{n} k_{ij}$ is the total consumption of commodity C_i by all owners and k the vector of k_i. In this aggregated version, however, unlike in $(3'')$, the connection between production and exchange is lost.

Certain simplifying assumptions underlie the shift from the general, but less precise formulations of (1), (2), and (3) to the specific, detailed formulations $(1')$, $(2')$, and $(3')$, and $(1'')$, $(2'')$, and $(3'')$. These may be grouped under the three headings of products, means of production, and labour.

Products. Formulation $(1')$ assumes a one-to-one correspondence between production processes and products. In other words, each process manufactures only one product (no joint-production), and each product is manufactured through one production process alone (no choice of technique). In particular, the manufacture of durable means of production, such as machines (which can be treated as a special case of joint production), has not been considered.

The formulation $(2')$ assumes a one-to-one correspondence of production processes (and hence products) and owners. Each production process has only one owner, thus excluding forms of ownership such as joint-stock companies, and each owner owns a single production process, thus excluding multi-product enterprises and the related possibility of the use of means of production not obtained through the market.

Joint production (including durable machinery) and choice of technique can both be brought into the analysis by assuming that there are m production processes, each producing n commodities. The representation of production as $(\text{diag } l, A) \rightarrow I$ would then be amended, the identity matrix I replaced by an $n \times m$ matrix B of joint products (to which A and diag l would have to be adjusted). This, however, would complicate not only the consideration of production, but also and even more the analysis of exchange and of the relation between them. (The classic example of joint production is the case of wool and mutton. A modern example might be the 'universal' joint product 'waste', which as far as I know has not yet been considered from this angle.)

Means of production. In (1') it is assumed that only (manufactured) products serve as means of production; land and landownership are therefore excluded. In addition, (1') also rests on the assumption that all products share the same length of production cycle (for example, one year), within which all means of production are fully used up and after which all products are simultaneously available for exchange. Without this assumption exchange could not be represented as in (2'), nor could the connection between production and exchange be expressed as a simple succession as in (3'). (This assumption is less important for the quantitative description of production in (1').) Constant returns to scale are assumed for (1''), and consequently for (3'') too.

Labour. Finally, in (1') it is assumed that only one type of labour is used in the manufacture of a product; the combination of various types of labour in single production processes is therefore not considered. (In short, the division of labour is regarded as mediated through the market, not the factory floor.) Homogeneous labour, customarily regarded as the norm, is admitted here as a limiting case. Differing types of labour within one production process could be dealt with by replacing the diag l in the representation of production (diag l, A) → I by a more general $m \times n$ matrix L.

The point of these assumptions is to free our central problem —investigation of the role of diverse labours from the standpoint of production, exchange, and their mutual interaction— from additional complications. (Even where labour is assumed to be homogeneous, joint production is a fairly complicated issue, with its own set of problems.[7])

The relations (1′), (2′), and (3′) serve as the basis for the subsequent analysis. They specify the basic model of an economic structure for a society in which distribution is effected through exchange and the products of labour take the form of commodities.

The relation (3′) formulates the link between the *use-structure* of commodities—given by P and K—and their *exchange-structure*, given by E. These structures are prerequisites for each other, but are also antithetical in certain respects. This will become evident when the role of labour and the proportioning of value in exchange are examined. Chapter 2 therefore begins with a closer investigation of the exchange-structure.

2
The Value-Form

One of the main features of a market economy stressed in chapter 1 was that the social mediation of separate and differing private labours is effected through the exchange of the products of labour. As this chapter will show, this requires that the products of labour assume the form of value in relation to one another. It is characteristic of this form that all those attributes that make products attractive or repulsive to individuals are socially relevant only to the extent that they are expressed in the *mutual relation of two products*. (This stands in contrast to 'primitive' societies, in which the relation of individuals or clans to the products of labour, or to each other, is of direct economic significance in the form of rites, mores, kinship, and so on; in a market economy, the accordance of such significance to kinship would be regarded as nepotism.)

The basic question to be considered is this: how can the form of value of commodities as a relation between two commodities be described with greater precision? The subject of the value-form remains to this day one of the central and controversial issues in political economy.[1]

The most important consequences of the answer offered here are:

—the determination of money, and hence the meaning of the expression 'the price of a commodity' (chapter 3);

—the derivation of a concept of 'abstract labour' (chapter 5) that subsequently underpins the rest of the study.

1. The Impossible Equation

Let us return once more to the exchange-structure. Let C_i be some particular commodity; if the production process is to continue, a certain quantity of this commodity must be exchanged for particular quantities of other commodities C_j ($j \neq i$). But the commodity in question will not be exchanged for two or more other commodities in a single act of exchange. Most often only two commodities will be involved in an act of exchange, so the exchange-structure consists of elementary *acts of exchange*, each involving two commodities. Regardless of why such acts of exchange take place, the salient fact here is that *when* they do a certain quantity of one product is exchanged for a certain quantity of the other. If we denote the commodities by A and B and the corresponding quantities by x and y, then the actual equating of the commodities in an act of exchange can be symbolized as $xA = yB$. Regarded merely as events, individual acts of exchange have no connection with one another and are simply fortuitous happenings. Two different acts of exchange are mutually independent and may differ in various respects. For example, exchanges of the same products may differ if they occur at different times or locations. Apples and pears may have exchanged at the ratio 2 : 1 in West Germany last year, and at 3 : 1 this year. The ratio in France at the same time may be 3 : 2. (Of course, exchange actually occurs in money, but the result is the equation of apples and pears in a certain proportion.) Nevertheless, acts of exchange that are otherwise identical cannot normally be differentiated by the participation of different individuals. As far as the exchange ratio of apples and pears is concerned, it is irrelevant whether the buyers are a cabinet minister, a miner, or a nun. The independence of acts of exchange in the sense that they involve different products is more important than their variety in time and space, of which we will take no further account. An example may clarify the point. Consider three products, A, B, and C, which are exchanged for one another in three independent acts of exchange, as follows.

Act 1. Exchange of A and B, where $xA = yB$.
Act 2. Exchange of B and C, where $uB = vC$.
Act 3. Exchange of A and C, where $wA = zC$.

Because of the independence of these acts of exchange, in general there will be no connection between the three exchange-ratios $\frac{y}{x}, \frac{v}{u}, \frac{z}{w}$. In particular, there is no reason to suppose that the relation $\frac{z}{w} = \frac{y}{x} \cdot \frac{v}{u}$ suggested by the use of the equals sign is valid. If b is the number of units of product B that exchange for one unit of product A, then $b = \frac{y}{x}$, and correspondingly $c = \frac{v}{u}, a = \frac{z}{w}$. The situation is briefly resumed in fig. 8, in which it is possible that $a \neq b \cdot c$.

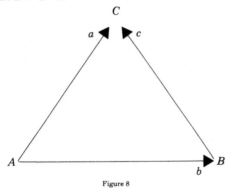

Figure 8

The fact that it may be that $a \neq b \cdot c$ contradicts the interpretation of '$xA = yB$' as an equation in the usual sense. To use an expression coined by Jacques Rancière, the relation $xA = yB$ amounts to an impossible equation.[2] The situation $a \neq b \cdot c$ expresses an inconsistency in the exchange-structure, as will soon become clear. Since the exchange-structure is consistent in reality—indeed, with regular exchange the proportions tend to acquire some fixity, as even a glimpse at the market will show—this reality would seem to require explanation. In other words, why is the impossible equation possible? Since merely unclear formulations are sometimes passed off as enlightening dialectics, a straightforward comment may be in order. The concise but paradoxical formulation of the above-mentioned situation as an impossible equation can be avoided by replacing the equals sign, '=', customarily used in political economy (but reserved in mathematics for numbers) with a neutral sign such as τ, which will denote the specific process of the equating of products in an act of exchange. The situation under consideration can now be rewritten as $A \tau bB, B \tau cC, A \tau aC$, whereby it is possible that $a \neq b \cdot c$. The outstanding problem is now: why is it that given $A \tau bB$ and $B \tau cC$ it necessarily follows that $A \tau (bc)C$? Reformulating the problem this way allows us to avoid the paradox of the non-applicability of the equals sign in the context of acts of exchange. (This also illustrates that prefabricated concepts intended for use in one sphere should not be allowed to generate their own meanings in quite different contexts. In the next paragraph it will become apparent that it is necessary to abandon the traditional equals sign completely.)

Let us return to the subject of the inconsistency of acts of exchange. If they are not consistent with one another, then one commodity-owner (at least) might profit through exchange alone. The following example illustrates the point. Consider three commodities, where $a = 8$, $b = 2$, $c = 3$. The owner of commodity A obtains 8 units of C for one unit of A in exchange between A and C, and $\frac{8}{3}$ units of B in exchange for these 8 units of C; if these are now exchanged for A again, the commodity-owner will acquire $\frac{8}{6}$ units of A. He will thus have obtained $\frac{4}{3}$ units of commodity A through exchanges of one initial unit of A, thus registering a profit of 33 per cent. Similar opportunities would be open to the owners of B and C. The process by which the owner of A made a gain is depicted in fig. 9. This profit is possible because the acts of exchange are inconsistent—that is, $8 \neq 2 \cdot 3$. Were it not for this inconsistency, none of the three owners could register a gain through exchange alone.

Consideration of the consequences of the inconsistency could be extended to any number of commodities. The situation is reasonably easy to follow with 3 commodities, since only 3 independent acts of exchange are being examined. As the number of commodities rises, the number of possible independent acts of

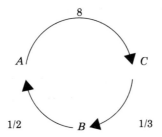

Figure 9

commodities. Four commodities potentially involve 6 independent acts of exchange; 5 involve 10 possible acts of exchange. In general, with n commodities the number of possible independent acts of exchange is equal to $\dfrac{n(n-1)}{2}$. Because of the independence of the acts of exchange—which rests on the mutually independent private labours and the mutually independent private ownership of the products—the exchange-structure linking the n commodities is not necessarily consistent. If C_1, $C_2, \ldots, C_n$ represent n commodities, and e_{ij} the number of units of commodity C_j that exchange for one unit of C_i (where $i \neq j$), then $e_{ji} = \dfrac{1}{e_{ij}}$, since whenever one unit of C_i is exchanged for e_{ij} units of C_j, one unit of C_j is simultaneously exchanged for e_{ji} units of C_i (see the above example involving 3 commodities). For the exchange-structure to be consistent in the case of three commodities C_i, C_j, and C_k, the relationship $e_{ij} = e_{ik} \cdot e_{kj}$ must hold.

An $n \times n$ matrix $E = (e_{ij})_{1 \leq i,j \leq n}$ for which $e_{ji} = \dfrac{1}{e_{ij}}$ will be called consistent if it meets the consistency requirement set out above. The logic is as follows: because of what they represent, the e_{ij} are neither negative nor zero, but are always positive. Since no commodity C_i exchanges with itself, the number e_{ii} is not defined. Without saying anything else about commodity exchange, then, we can stipulate that $e_{ii} = 1$ for every i. If the exchange-structure is consistent, the number e_{ij} is called the *exchange-value* of commodity C_i relative to C_j.

The situation described in the example of three commodities can be generalized. Indeed:

Proposition. The exchange-structure is consistent if and only if no commodity-owners can augment their stock of commodities through mere exchange.

Demonstration. That the owner of commodity C_i cannot augment one unit of this commodity through exchange alone means that for any assortment of commodities $C_{i_1}, C_{i_2}, \ldots, C_{i_r}$ with $1 \leq r \leq n$

$$e_{ii_1} \cdot e_{i_1 i_2} \cdots \cdot e_{i_r i} \leq 1. \qquad (*)$$

(This corresponds to circular exchange, as in the three-commodity diagram above.) If the exchange-structure is consistent, then repeated application of the consistency requirement will yield the relation (*). Conversely, if (*) is the case, then for $i_1 = j$, $i_2 = k$, $e_{ij} \cdot e_{jk} \cdot e_{ki} \leq 1$. Since (*) applies for every commodity-owner, this inequality will apply to all indices i, j, k between 1 and n, and therefore $e_{kj} \cdot e_{ji} \cdot e_{ik} \leq 1$. Since for two indices a and b, $e_{ab} = \dfrac{1}{e_{ba}}$, it follows from both inequalities that $e_{ij} \cdot e_{jk} \leq e_{ik}$ $\leq e_{ij} \cdot e_{jk}$, which fulfils the consistency requirement. This proves the proposition.

(It is possible to make a profit through mere exchange through currency speculation on an international scale. Internationally, then, the exchange-structure need not be consistent.)

If no commodity-owners can augment their stocks through mere exchange in a given exchange-structure, then exchange within this structure may be called *equivalent-exchange*. As an initial result, simple but of considerable importance, we may therefore note:

Conclusion. An exchange-structure is consistent if and only if exchange within it is equivalent-exchange.

In contrast to a commonly held view (see the bulk of the literature cited in note 1 of this chapter), equivalence as defined here relates *not* to a single individual act of exchange, but to the exchange-structure as a whole. In particular, the equivalence of two quantities of commodities does *not* mean that they embody an equal amount of labour-time or something similar. The term 'equivalent exchange' can be applied to an individual act of exchange only if it is one act of a structure of equivalent-exchange. (The exchange between pears and apples, for example, may be equivalent in one society but not in another.) [3]

In a society based on exchange in which capital is used productively, exchange, the principle of social intercourse, must be equivalent exchange (see chapter 6, section 3). But the exchange-structure is not automatically consistent, but rather implies the possibility of inconsistency: its shape is examined in what follows. [4]

2. The Value Relation

Up to now, inconsistency has been considered in the context of actual exchange ratios, it being assumed that every commodity is exchanged for every other commodity in one act of exchange. This procedure is unsatisfactory, for a number of reasons. For an act of exchange between two commodities C_i and C_j to take place, the commodity C_j must possess a use-value for the owner of C_i, and C_i a use-value for the owner of C_j. Such an exchange, under conditions of a 'double coincidence of wants', will be called a *direct exchange*. So far we have assumed that direct exchange was possible between all commodities, for only then could the exchange-matrix E of the elements $e_{ij} > 0$ be defined. In general, however, direct exchange between any two given commodities is not possible, and where the division of labour is very pronounced such an occurrence would in fact be very rare. The general reason for this is that the use-structure and exchange-structure are quite different and not necessarily coincident forms. In short, there is a contradiction between use and exchange by virtue of their inner structure. To fill out this laconic formulation, let us return to the discussion of exchange in chapter 1. By definition, y_{ij} is the amount of C_i that the owner of C_j wishes to acquire; exchange between C_i and C_j thus has the form

$$C_i \underset{y_{ji}}{\overset{y_{ij}}{\rightleftharpoons}} C_j$$

A direct exchange is possible if and only if $y_{ij} > 0$ *and* $y_{ji} > 0$. In that case one unit of C_i will exchange for $e_{ij} = \dfrac{y_{ji}}{y_{ij}}$ units of C_j. As can be seen, $e_{ij} > 0$ and $e_{ji} = \dfrac{1}{e_{ij}}$. The situation considered in chapter 1 thus holds if and only if $Y > 0$. However, $y_{ij} = k_{ij} + \bar{y}_{ij}$ $= k_{ij} + a_{ij}\bar{y}_j$, and thus $y_{ij} > 0$ if and only if $k_{ij} > 0$ or $a_{ij} > 0$ (or k_{ij} $+ a_{ij} > 0$), assuming that $\bar{y}_j > 0$ for all j, i.e. that exactly the same commodities are manufactured once again after exchange occurs.

In short, $Y > 0$ if and only if $A + K > 0$. Now, for many pairs of commodities it will indeed be the case that $a_{ij} + k_{ij} = 0$; for example, if C_i and C_j are not means of consumption, then $k_{ij} = k_{ji}$ $= 0$, while if C_i is a means of production for C_j but not vice versa, $a_{ij} > 0$ and $a_{ji} = 0$; although $a_{ij} + k_{ij} > 0$, the other relation yields a_{ji} $+ k_{ji} = 0$, which means that no direct exchange between C_i and C_j is possible. If E denotes the matrix in which in position (i, j), $i \neq j$, we have e_{ij} when a direct exchange is possible between C_i and C_j, and which contains ones in the diagonal but zeros elsewhere (thus generalizing the earlier definition), then the situation can be summarized as follows: exchange, given by the matrix E, and use, given by the matrices A and K (where A depicts the structure of production and K the structure of consumption), generally possess different structures. Any zero in $A + K$ is also a zero in the corresponding place in E, but the converse is not true; E thus generally has more zeros (in terms of occupancy of the matrix) than $A + K$ (in other words, it is more weakly occupied).

This situation can be examined with greater precision with the aid of the concept of a chain within a matrix (see mathematical appendix, part 1). A chain is said to exist between i and j *through exchange* if there are r different indices $i_1, i_2, \ldots, i_r$ such that $e_{ii_1} > 0$, $e_{i_1 i_2} > 0, \ldots, e_{i_r j} > 0$. In the case of the matrix Y of the y_{ij}, the chain from i to j is defined *through use* (and correspondingly for A for production and K for consumption). Every chain established through exchange necessarily presupposes a chain through use (with the same indices), but not every chain through use implies a chain through exchange that could realize it. In other words, if the E-matrix is connected, then the Y and $A + K$ matrices will also be connected, but the converse is not necessarily true (see below for an example). An *indirect* exchange is said to exist between C_i and C_j if there is a chain from i to j through exchange. Indirect exchange therefore consists of a series of direct acts of exchange. If all acts of exchange are direct, then an indirect exchange is possible between all commodities (not uniquely determined), which corresponds to direct exchange for all commodities, if and only if the exchange-structure is consistent. As already emphasized, in general direct exchange between two commodities is not possible, and although indirect exchange may be possible, this is by no means always the case, as will be shown in an example below. In the subsequent analysis it is assumed that at least one indirect exchange is possible between any two (different) commodities; in other words, that E is connected (or irreducible; see mathematical appendix, part 1).[5] It is then possible to define a relation τ on the set of all quantities of commodities $C_1, \ldots, C_n$, that is, on $C = \{xC_i \mid x > 0, 1 \leq i \leq n\}$, as follows: $xC_i \tau yC_j$ if and only if an indirect exchange exists from i to j, thus there exist $i_1, \ldots, i_r$ such that $e_{ii_1} > 0, \ldots, e_{i_r j} > 0$ and such that $\frac{y}{x} = e_{ii_1} \ldots e_{i_r j}$. Since in general there are more possibilities for indirect exchange, let *one* of these be selected for each pair (i, j). The *relation of indirect exchange* τ has the following properties.

1. It is *complete*. In other words: for any two commodities C_i and C_j, there are positive quantities x and y such that $xC_i \tau yC_j$.

2. It is *one-one*. That is:

    if $xC_i \tau 1C_j$ and $yC_i \tau 1C_j$, then $x = y$.

3. It is *homogeneous*. That is:

    if $xC_i \tau yC_j$ and $a > 0$, then $(ax)C_i \tau (ay)C_j$.

4. It is *reflexive*. That is:

    $1C_i \tau 1C_i$, for every i.

(Completeness follows from the supposition that E is irreducible; τ must be one-one because of the selection of exactly one indirect exchange opportunity from i to j; homogeneity follows directly from the definition of τ, and reflexivity from the convention that $e_{ii} = 1$ for all i.)

In general, the relation of indirect exchange is *neither symmetric nor transitive*. Symmetry means that if $xC_i \, \tau \, yC_j$, then $yC_j \, \tau \, xC_i$. Because of completeness, indirect exchange possibilities exist such that $\frac{y}{x} = e_{ii_1} \ldots e_{i_r j}$ and $\frac{x}{y} = e_{jj_1} \ldots e_{j_s i}$. Because of the symmetry of direct exchange, it follows from the first of these expressions that $\frac{x}{y} = e_{i_1 i} \ldots e_{j i_r} = e_{j i_r} \ldots e_{i_1 i}$, but since in general there are more opportunities for indirect exchange, the chain $(j_1, \ldots, j_s)$ of j to i does not necessarily coincide with the chain $(i_r, \ldots, i_1)$ of i to j, which is the reverse of the chain $(i_1, \ldots, i_r)$; they can differ as regards their length $(r \neq s)$ and, even if they have the same length, as regards the individual points of exchange $(j_1 \neq i_r$, etc.)

Consider the following illustration. Given the definition of τ, select a minimal chain from i to j (that is, the chain for which the expression $e_{ii_1} \ldots e_{i_r j}$ is smaller than for any other chain); then symmetry between C_i and C_j would imply that this chain is also maximal—that is, that the value $e_{ii_1} \ldots e_{i_r j}$ is exceeded by no other chain. Symmetry between C_i and C_j would thus mean that this expression would be identical for all connections of i to j, which in general is not to be expected.

In contrast to direct exchange, which is indeed symmetric $(e_{ij} = \frac{1}{e_{ji}})$, indirect exchange is in general not symmetric. But neither direct nor indirect exchange need be transitive, even if all acts of exchange could be direct. In that case $1C_i \, \tau \, e_{ij} \, C_j$, $1C_i \, \tau \, e_{ik} \, C_k$, and $1C_k \, \tau \, e_{kj} \, C_j$. If this relation were transitive, then it would follow that $1C_i \, \tau \, e_{ik} \cdot e_{kj} \, C_j$; that is, $e_{ij} = e_{ik} \cdot e_{kj}$, which is not necessarily the case, since direct exchange may be inconsistent.

A simple example will serve both to illustrate this point and to call attention to a new problem. For a weaver to produce linen, thread, which is produced by a spinner, is required. The linen is made into shirts by a tailor, and the shirts are consumed by all three. The linkage between the commodities used, in both production and consumption, is therefore such that the third commodity is relevant to the relationship between the other two. This use-structure can by symbolized as in fig. 10.

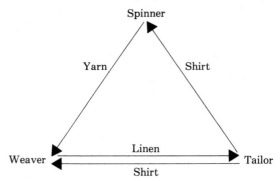

Figure 10

Since shirts (C_3) are the only means of consumption but are not means of production, and since thread (C_1) and cloth (C_2) are the means of production, production and consumption can be depicted as follows (since the intent is merely to represent structure, positive quantities are simply marked thus: +).

$$A = \begin{bmatrix} 0 & + & 0 \\ 0 & 0 & + \\ 0 & 0 & 0 \end{bmatrix} \quad K = \begin{bmatrix} 0 & 0 & 0 \\ 0 & 0 & 0 \\ + & + & + \end{bmatrix} \quad A + K = \begin{bmatrix} 0 & + & 0 \\ 0 & 0 & + \\ + & + & + \end{bmatrix}$$

Both the production-structure and the consumption-structure are non-connected (reducible) in themselves, but the overall use-structure, whose chains are given by $A + K$, is connected (irreducible). The only direct exchange possible is between shirts and cloth. If $x = e_{23}$, then the matrix of possible direct exchange has the configuration

$$E = \begin{bmatrix} 1 & 0 & 0 \\ 0 & 1 & x \\ 0 & \frac{1}{x} & 1 \end{bmatrix}$$

This matrix is *not* connected. It has already been noted that when the use-structure is non-connected, the exchange-structure is also likely to be non-connected. This example shows that such a situation can crop up in other cases too. Since only one act of direct exchange is possible, real indirect exchange cannot exist at all, and no relation of indirect exchange can be defined (in other words, indirect exchange is not complete).

Clearly, in a society based on exchange, direct exchange is not an adequate principle of social intercourse, because the required double-coincidence of wants occurs so rarely; indirect exchange is therefore a necessity. But although it is necessary, the above example demonstrates that it is not sufficient, given certain use-structures, to permit the necessary transactions—namely when there are 'too few' acts of direct exchange through which indirect exchange can take place. Nevertheless, the example presented above—and, in general, any society based on exchange—requires the development of exchange-transactions as a prerequisite for further production, and therefore for the preservation of that society. It is therefore necessary that commodities be placed in a social relationship that makes the required circulation of commodities possible. (This circulation, and in particular its operation in the above example, will be examined more closely in the next chapter, when we deal with money. What if forms of social cooperation other than exchange were permitted in the above example?)

In the subsequent analysis it is assumed that such a relationship between commodities does exist. This is always trivially the case when the use-structure, and especially the production-structure and consumption-structure, is strictly positive (that is, when $A + K > 0$, or in other words when $A > 0$ or $K > 0$). As the previous discussion demonstrated, such a relation also exists if the exchange-structure is connected (the E-matrix of direct exchange is connected), since in that case the indirect exchange relation patterned after τ constitutes such a relation. The discussion of the relation of indirect exchange showed that such a relation has the properties 1-4, but usually not symmetry and transitivity. At this point, reversing our direction of approach, we will postulate that this sort of relation between commodities, which may be called the value relation, exists. More precisely: a binary relation R on the set of quantities of

commodities $C = \{xC_i \mid x > 0, 1 \leq i \leq n\}$ possessing the properties specified in 1-4 above is called the value relation or the
value-form.

The meaning of the value relation R is as follows: $xC_i \, R \, yC_j$
states that a certain quantity x of commodity C_i is set in relation to a certain quantity y of commodity C_j by the commodity-
owners engaged in exchange, and thus, in a certain sense, that
C_i is socially measured in terms of C_j. In short: x units of C_i are
(socially) worth y units of C_j. The activities of the owners consist in the exchange of the commodities—with each transaction
comprising a large number of moments, such as knowledge and
calculation, but hopes and fears as well. It is *characteristic* of
this relation that:

It is an *objective relation*—a relation between objects, commodities, in particular quantities. Although this relation may
involve quite diverse subjective conceptions of the utility of
these commodities, such factors are not analysed as such here,
and are considered only to the extent that they influence the
relation between the quantities of the commodities. (The pivotal
point is thus neither the relation of the subject to commodities,
as in the concept of utility in subjective theories of value, nor
the relation between the subjects, as in the concept of power in
transaction theories.)

It is a *social relation* embracing all commodities and all the
commodity-owners involved in exchanging them. ('All' in the
sense implied by C. The relation of R to $xC_i \, R \, yC_j$ is similar to
the relation between a space and the distance between two
definite points in this space.)

It is a *piece-wise relation*; in other words, its social nature is
made up of binary links (pairings) between objects.

The completeness of R as defined in 1 above states that every
commodity stands in a value relation to every other—which
could be regarded as intrinsic to the very idea of a commodity.
(Nonetheless, not everything can be exchanged, even in a
society of exchange. If the set C includes products that cannot
be placed in the relation R to the other products, these will

simply be disregarded as not commodities.) That R is one-one (property 2) simply means that if two apples are worth one pear, then three apples cannot also be worth one pear. Homogeneity (3), expressed equally simply, states that if two apples are worth one pear, then four apples are worth two pears (there is, as it were, no bulk-discount). Finally, reflexivity (4) is a convention that does not impinge on the truth-value of any genuine propositions about different commodities.

Returning to the impossible equation, it is now possible to say that the ordinary equality relation "$=$" for numbers is a binary relation on the set of all numbers possessing the properties 1-4. However, the relation of equality has additional properties too, such as symmetry and transitivity, that are in general not possessed by the value relation, as shown in connection with the indirect-exchange relation τ. This can be formulated as follows: in the expression of value $xC_i \ R \ yC_j$, the commodities C_i and C_j play quite different roles: C_j is the standard of measurement by which the social value of C_i is measured (through the actions of individuals). In the expression of value $yC_j \ R \ xC_i$, these roles are reversed, and there is no reason (as yet) to suggest that both expressions describe the same state of affairs. In order to depict the value relation's lack of symmetry, the commodity C_i may be said to be in the *relative form of value* in the expression $xC_i \ R \ yC_j$ (it counts as value relative to another commodity), while C_j is in the *equivalent-form* (it serves as the equivalent, or better, the measure of value). There are therefore two ways in which a commodity can come into relation to all other commodities. First, one unit of a particular commodity can count as value in relation to all other quantities of commodities. This variant, which can be formally represented by the mapping $yC_j \rightarrow 1C_i \ R \ yC_j$ defined on the set C, is the *expanded value-form* of C_i. Second, all other commodities can express their value in one unit of a particular commodity. This variant, formally represented by the mapping $xC_i \rightarrow xC_i \ R \ 1C_j$ defined on C, is known as the *general value-form* of C_j. Personalized in terms of the commodity-owners, we may say that the general value-form of C_j represents the 'price system' of the owner of C_j in relation to all other commodities. The overall value-form R

therefore represents the various mutually competing, and not necessarily consistent, 'price systems'.

Since one and the same commodity can assume two different roles in the value-relation, there is no reason to suppose that transitivity will be a general feature of this relation. The expressions $xC_i R yC_j$ and $yC_j R zC_k$ do not imply any particular results, in particular not the expression $xC_i R zC_k$, since in $xC_i R yC_j$, C_j is in the equivalent form, but in $yC_j R zC_k$ it is in the relative form (on the basis of homogeneity). To infer transitivity, then, it would be necessary that a transition exist from the equivalent to the relative value-form of the commodity C_j.

3. The Problem of Transitivity

A binary relation that is reflexive, symmetric, and transitive is called an *equivalence relation*. An equivalence relation is quite close to the relation of equality, but nevertheless differs from it in a number of respects. It is now crucial to examine whether the value relation R is an equivalence relation—in particular whether it is transitive, and if so, why.

In the passage dealing with the impossible equation, it was shown that exchange through direct acts of exchange constitutes equivalent-exchange if and only if the exchange matrix is consistent. An analogous proposition also applies in the more general case of the value-relation. Namely:

For a value-relation R on C there exist uniquely determined positive numbers z_{ij} such that $1C_i R z_{ij} C_j$ for all $i, j = 1, \ldots, n$.

Demonstration. Since R is complete, for C_i and C_j there exist positive numbers x and y such that $xC_i R yC_j$. Since R is homogeneous, $1C_i R \frac{y}{x} C_j$, where $\frac{y}{x} > 0$. Conversely, consider any number $z > 0$ such that $1C_i R zC_j$. Since R is homogeneous, $\frac{1}{z}C_i R 1C_j$ and also $\frac{x}{y}C_i R 1C_j$. Also, since R is one-one, $\frac{1}{z} = \frac{x}{y}$, and hence $z = \frac{y}{x}$. Thus for C_i and C_j there exists a unique positive number z_{ij} such that $1C_i R z_{ij} C_j$.

Since R is reflexive, $1C_i\,R\,1C_i$ and $z_{ii} = 1$. And since the coefficients z_{ij} depict both direct and indirect exchange (see the discussion of the indirect-exchange relation), and thus the process of the circulation of commodities, the matrix Z of the z_{ij} may be called the *circulation matrix*. (For more on circulation, see chapter 3.)

The following propositions establish a connection between the value relation and the circulation-matrix.

Proposition 1. The value relation R is symmetric if and only if for any two commodities C_i and C_j, $z_{ji} = \frac{1}{z_{ij}}$.

Demonstration. Let R be symmetric. If $1C_i\,R\,z_{ij}\,C_j$, then $z_{ij}\,C_j$ $R\,1C_i$. Since R is homogeneous (by definition), $1C_j\,R\,\frac{1}{z_{ij}}\,C_i$. Since $1C_j\,R\,z_{ji}\,C_i$ and since R is one-one, it follows that $z_{ji} = \frac{1}{z_{ij}}$.

Conversely, let Z have this property. If $xC_i\,R\,yC_j$, then by homogeneity, $1C_i\,R\,\frac{y}{x}\,C_j$. Since $1C_i\,R\,z_{ij}\,C_j$ and since R is one-one, it follows that $z_{ij} = \frac{y}{x}$. Hence $z_{ji} = \frac{1}{z_{ij}} = \frac{x}{y}$. Since $1C_j\,R$ $z_{ji}\,C_i$, it follows that $1C_j\,R\,\frac{x}{y}\,C_i$, and by homogeneity it follows that $yC_j\,R\,xC_i$. The value relation is therefore symmetric.

Since the value relation is not necessarily symmetric, in circulation, unlike in direct exchange, z_{ji} may be different from $\frac{1}{z_{ij}}$. (In the case of the exchange of money, this actually happens: the exchange-rate between two currencies depends on which is being changed into which).

It was stated above that a matrix $Z = (z_{ij})$, $1 \leq i, j \leq n$, such that $z_{ji} = \frac{1}{z_{ij}}$ is consistent if for any three different commodities C_i, C_j, C_k

$$z_{ij} = z_{ik} \cdot z_{kj} \qquad (*)$$

Since $z_{ii} = 1$ in the circulation matrix, $z_{ji} = \frac{1}{z_{ij}}$ is equivalent to $z_{ii} = z_{ij} \cdot z_{ji}$, and for all i and j this is equivalent to (*) for the three commodities, of which two are identical. The circulation matrix Z is therefore consistent if and only if it possesses property (*), where these indices can also be identical. After this digression, we may note:

Proposition 2. The value relation is transitive if and only if the circulation matrix is consistent.

Demonstration. Let R be transitive. Then $1C_k R z_{kj} C_j$, and by homogeneity, $z_{ik} C_k R z_{ik} z_{kj} C_j$. Since $1C_i R z_{ik} C_k$, it follows from the transitivity of R that $1C_i R z_{ik} \cdot z_{kj} C_j$. Since $1C_i R z_{ij} C_j$, and since R is homogeneous and one-one, it follows that $z_{ij} = z_{ik} \cdot z_{kj}$. Since two indices can coincide in this expression, Z is consistent. Conversely, let Z be consistent and let $xC_i R yC_k$ and $yC_k R zC_j$. Since R is homogeneous and one-one, it follows that $z_{ik} = \dfrac{y}{x}$ and $z_{kj} = \dfrac{z}{y}$. Hence, $z_{ij} = z_{ik} \cdot z_{kj} = \dfrac{y}{x} \cdot \dfrac{z}{y} = \dfrac{z}{x}$. Since $1C_i R z_{ij} C_j$, it follows from homogeneity that $xC_i R zC_j$. R is therefore transitive.

These two propositions yield:

Proposition 3. If the value relation is transitive, then it is necessarily symmetric as well.

Demonstration. If R is transitive, then Proposition 2 tells us that Z is consistent. In particular, $z_{ji} = \dfrac{1}{z_{ij}}$ for any two commodities C_i and C_j. By Proposition 1, R is therefore symmetric.

On the basis of this proposition, we may state that the value relation is an equivalence relation if and only if it is transitive. In other words, once the transitivity of R is determined, the question of whether it is an equivalence relation is settled as well. Moreover, the proposition implies that transitivity is not an automatic property of R, since R is not automatically symmetric.

Since the value relation is not inherently transitive, and thus not inherently an equivalence relation either, we are confronted with what may be called the transitivity problem (or, the equivalence problem): what is the basis for the transitivity, and consequently the symmetry, of the value relation?

The question of whether exchange ratios are consistent given the independence of acts of exchange, which was discussed in the section on the impossible equation, now appears, in the light of the value relation, as the question of whether this relation is transitive in view of the fact that a commodity can assume contradictory roles within it.

The formulation of the value relation R and its properties, along with the various propositions, has answered the question posed at the beginning of this chapter. But a new question has simultaneously arisen: that of the transitivity of R.

The result of this chapter, which will be referred back to subsequently, can be summarized as follows.

The following propositions are logically equivalent.

1. The value relation is transitive.

2. The value relation is an equivalence relation.

3. The circulation matrix is consistent.

4. Commodity-owners cannot augment their property through the mere exchange of commodities (exchange is thus equivalent-exchange).

(The equivalence of 3 and 4 follows in the same way as the corresponding propositions for the exchange matrix E.) The *how* of value—namely, the value-*form*, which means the value *relation*—is thus clarified. The *what* of value, namely its content, will be considered later, when we discuss labour. But the next chapter must first examine how the transitivity of the value relation becomes objective at the level of things themselves, in the shape of money.

3
Money and the
Price-Form

Money exists, and has existed, in a variety of concrete forms, ranging from cattle to gold coins to the European Currency Unit.[1] Theories of the functions and essence of money are no less plentiful, extending even to the question of why money exists at all. The profusion of disparate theories of money suggests that there is no theory of money yet.

This chapter will focus on a question raised by the points made in the previous chapter. Although simple, it has received the most divergent answers: to what extent does money as a commodity play a special role in relation to all other commodities, and how can this role be described with greater precision?

In some respects the analysis that follows takes up Marx's discussion of money in the framework of his analysis of the value-form; in others it builds on some recent contributions to the micro-economic foundations of monetary theory.[2] The essence of my point of view is that money should be treated not as a mere magnitude, but as a structure. This aspect of money, I would argue, has so far been neglected.

1.   The Structure of Money

Intuitively a money-commodity will be a commodity that serves both as the measure for all other commodities and as a medium for the circulation of commodities. (The limited scope of the basic question raised above excludes money's possible role as a so-called store of value.)

A given system of commodity exchange may have a single money-commodity or several, up to a limiting case in which all commodities are money-commodities.

To be more precise, a system of commodity-exchange is here regarded as a certain relation between quantities of commodities, in other words, a relation τ on the set of commodities $C = \{xC_i \mid x > 0 \ 1 \leq i \leq n\}$. (As before, for the sake of brevity we will write $C_i = 1C_i$ for the commodity C_i or for one unit quantity of this commodity, depending on the context.) To represent interchanges such as direct exchange itself as a relation such as τ, we must consider relations τ that are more general than value relations (although τ is still a binary relation.)

For a commodity C_k we may define as follows the relation τ_k *induced* by the commodity C_k:

$xC_i \ \tau_k \ yC_j$ if and only if there exists a $v > 0$ such that $xC_i \ \tau \ vC_k$ and $yC_j \ \tau \ vC_k$.

Intuitively: the relation τ_k holds between two quantities of commodities if both can be expressed in the same quantity of C_k. (If the general form of value for τ is considered, as in the case of the value relation, it will be seen that the relation induced by C_k arises directly from the general form of value of C_k.)

A commodity C_k is called a measure or *equivalent* (in relation to τ) if τ_k is a transitive relation. Intuitively: the quantities of the other commodities will be completely and consistently expressed in quantities of the equivalent. A commodity C_k is called a *means of circulation* (in relation to τ) if it is the case that: $xC_i \ \tau_k \ yC_j$ holds if and only if there exists a $u > 0$ such that $xC_i \ \tau \ uC_k$ and $uC_k \ \tau \ yC_j$. (Clearly, if τ is symmetric, any equivalent will also be a means of circulation.) Intuitively: two quantities of commodities will be expressed in the same quantity of C_k if and only if they are circulated through an identical quantity of C_k.

A commodity C_k may thus be called a *money-commodity* (in relation to τ) if it is both an equivalent and a means of circulation (in relation to τ). This definition amounts to a more precise formulation of what a money-commodity was intuitively considered to be. If C_k is a money-commodity, then τ_k is a *money relation*. If C_k is a money-commodity and if for another commodity C_i it is the case that $xC_i \tau vC_k$ for some quantities $x, v > 0$, then we will say that C_i stands in the *price-form* relative to the money-commodity (C_i stands in the relative value-form, C_k in the equivalent form). By definition, a money commodity C_k is always linked to a transitive value relation, and since τ_k is symmetric by definition, the induced relation τ_k is also an equivalence relation. Consequently, no commodity-owners can augment their stocks in relation to τ_k (chapter 2). However, as we will soon see, τ and τ_k generally differ and can coincide only if τ itself is already an equivalence relation. The existence of a money-commodity therefore does not solve the problem of transitivity, although it does make it possible to describe a consistent system of commodity interchange through the money relation τ_k.

If τ is a homogeneous, one-one relation on C, then it can be expressed in a matrix Z as follows (see chapter 2 and the mathematical appendix for the various properties of relations). Let C_i and C_j be two commodities; if there exist $x > 0$, $y > 0$ such that $xC_i \tau yC_j$, let $z_{ij} = \dfrac{y}{x}$, otherwise $z_{ij} = 0$. Since τ is homogeneous and one-one, Z is uniquely determined. Conversely, if Z is an $n \times n$ matrix whose elements are 0 or positive, then we can associate with it a definite homogeneous and one-one relation τ: $xC_i \tau yC_j$ if and only if $z_{ij} > 0$ and $\dfrac{y}{x} = z_{ij}$.

Let τ be a homogeneous, one-one relation, and Z the associated matrix. Then the following properties apply to the connection between the two.

(a) τ is reflexive if and only if $z_{ii} = 1$ for all i.

(b) τ is symmetric if and only if $z_{ji} = \dfrac{1}{z_{ij}}$ for $z_{ij} > 0$.

(c) τ is transitive if and only if for any three commodities and for positive z_{ik} and z_{kj}: $z_{ij} = z_{ik} \cdot z_{kj}$.

(d) τ is complete if and only if $z_{ij} > 0$ for all i, j.

(See the discussion of the value relation in the previous chapter).

Let us take a first example: *direct exchange*. Let τ be the direct-exchange relation, that is, the relation that, under the conditions described above, is associated with the exchange matrix E defined in the previous chapter (where $e_{ij} > 0$ if and only if there is direct exchange between C_i and C_j; $e_{ii} = 1$, and $e_{ij} = 0$ otherwise). τ is homogeneous, one-one, and reflexive and symmetric. Since τ is symmetric, C_k is a money-commodity if and only if τ_k is a transitive value relation. Consequently, $xC_i \, \tau_k \, yC_j$ if and only if there exists a $v > 0$ such that $\frac{v}{x} = e_{ik}$, $\frac{v}{y} = e_{jk}$; in other words, if and only if $\frac{y}{x} = e_{ik} \cdot e_{kj}$ (and this expression is positive). If τ_k is complete, then the matrix of $z_{ij} = e_{ik} \cdot e_{kj}$ is positive, consistent, and contains only ones along its diagonal; τ_k is then a transitive value relation. C_k is therefore a money-commodity if and only if τ_k is complete, which means on the basis of the symmetry of τ: for every i, $e_{ik} > 0$. Thus, C_k is a money-commodity (in relation to τ, under direct exchange) if and only if direct-exchange is possible between C_k and every other commodity.[3] Consequently, at least one (or exactly one) money-commodity exists if and only if E has at least one (or exactly one) positive column (or row). There may be several money-commodities, and all commodities are money-commodities if and only if $E > 0$.

The arguments put forward in this example are valid more generally, as shown in the following propositions.

Proposition 1. If τ is a homogeneous one-one relation, then for any k, the induced relation τ_k is homogeneous, one-one, symmetric, and transitive. And the relation τ_k is complete if and only if it is reflexive.

Demonstration. That τ_k is symmetric follows immediately from the definition. That it is homogeneous follows from the homogeneity of τ. That it is one-one: let $xC_i \, \tau_k \, 1C_j$ and $yC_i \, \tau_k \, 1C_j$. Then $xC_i \, \tau \, vC_k$ and $yC_i \, \tau \, uC_k$; $1C_j \, \tau \, vC_k$ and $1C_j \, \tau \, uC_k$, where $u, v > 0$. Now, since τ is homogeneous and one-one, it follows that $\frac{x}{v} = \frac{y}{u}$ and that $u = v$; hence $x = y$. τ_k is therefore one-one. As for transitivity: if Z is the matrix of τ and $\overline{Z}$ the matrix of τ_k, then the positive elements of $\overline{Z}$ have the form $\bar{z}_{ij} = \frac{z_{ik}}{z_{jk}}$. Thus for positive elements, $\bar{z}_{il} \cdot \bar{z}_{1j} = \bar{z}_{ij}$, and τ_k is therefore transitive. Finally, τ_k is complete if and only if $z_{ik} > 0$ for every i, which is equivalent to $\bar{z}_{ii} = 1$ for all i. Hence the relation τ_k is complete if and only if it is reflexive.

The following proposition characterizes money-commodities for given relations τ.

Proposition 2. Let τ be a homogeneous, one-one, symmetric relation. Then C_k is a money-commodity (under τ) if and only if every quantity of commodities is expressed in a quantity of C_k; in other words, if for every C_i there exists a $v > 0$ such that $1 C_i \tau$ $v C_k$.

Demonstration. If C_k is a money-commodity, it trivially follows that any quantity of commodities can be expressed in a quantity of C_k. Conversely, if any quantity of commodities can be expressed in a quantity of C_k, then because of the symmetry and homogeneity of τ, τ_k is complete. By Proposition 1, τ_k is then a transitive value relation, and C_k is therefore an equivalent. Since τ is symmetric, C_k is also a means of circulation and hence a money-commodity.

We may now examine a further example: *indirect exchange.* Using the exchange matrix E for acts of direct exchange, a matrix $\overline{E}$ for indirect exchange may be constructed as follows: if $i \neq j$, and if there is a chain from i to j, then select a chain $e_{ii_1} > 0$, $e_{i_1i_2} > 0, \ldots, e_{i_rj}$. Then set $\bar{e}_{ij} = e_{ii_1} \cdot e_{i_1i_2} \cdots e_{i_rj}$ and $\bar{e}_{ji} = e_{ji_r} \cdots e_{i_2i_1} \cdot e_{i_1i}$. If there is no chain from i to j, then let $\bar{e}_{ij} = 0$. Finally, let $\bar{e}_{ii} = e_{ii} = 1$ for all i. Let τ be the homogeneous, one-one relation associated with $\overline{E}$. $\bar{\tau}$ is reflexive and symmetric (in contrast to the indirect-exchange relation discussed in chapter 2, the relation $\bar{\tau}$ is symmetric since the chain selected from j to i was in fact the inverse of the chain from i to j). By Proposition 2, then, C_k is a money-commodity (in relation to $\bar{\tau}$, namely under indirect exchange) if and only if for every i, $\bar{e}_{ki} > 0$ (or $\bar{e}_{ik} > 0$), that is, if C_k is linked to every other commodity through direct exchange. Thus, there exists a money-commodity if and only if the matrix E is connected. Now, if C_k is a money-commodity, then there is a chain from C_j to C_k, expressed in the term $\bar{e}_{jk}$, and a chain from C_k to C_i, expressed in the term $\bar{e}_{ki}$; a chain therefore exists from C_j to C_i (composed of those in $\bar{e}_{jk}$ and $\bar{e}_{ki}$), namely $\bar{e}_{ji} > 0$, although in general $\bar{e}_{ji} \neq \bar{e}_{jk} \cdot \bar{e}_{ki}$ (when the selected chain $\bar{e}_{ji}$ does not coincide with the composite chain). Hence, if a money-commodity exists (in relation to $\bar{\tau}$), then all commodities must be money-commodities; the relation $\bar{\tau}$ is thus a symmetric value relation, but is not necessarily transitive. This situation—in which either no money-commodity exists or else all commodities are money-commodities—does not necessarily arise if we abandon the general indirect-exchange relation described above and consider instead graduated indirect-exchange relations, in which the number of steps of indirect exchange is taken into account. An indirect-exchange relation of s steps would then be based on chains of the configuration $e_{ii_1} > 0$, $e_{i_1 i_2} > 0, \ldots, e_{i_r j} > 0$, where $r \leq s$. The direct-exchange relation and the general indirect-exchange relation are thus limiting cases of a graduated indirect-exchange relation, of any number of steps from zero upwards. The concept of a money-commodity under indirect-exchange is formally reminiscent of Sraffa's concept of a basic product. The former relates to commodity circulation (the E matrix), the latter to commodity production (the A matrix). (Although because of the symmetric definition of the E matrix, the money-commodity is subject to an all-or-nothing effect that is absent for basic products).

The two examples indicate on the one hand that a money-commodity may exist but need not and on the other hand that in the limiting case all commodities can be money-commodities. In general, the following holds.

Proposition 3. Let τ be a homogeneous and one-one relation. Then all commodities are money-commodities (under τ) if and only if τ is a symmetric value relation.

Demonstration. If τ is a symmetric value relation, then by

Proposition 2, all commodities are money-commodities. Conversely, let all commodities be money-commodities. Then all induced relations τ_k for $k = 1, 2, \ldots, n$ are complete, and τ is therefore also complete. Moreover, τ_k is reflexive for all k, and hence $xC_k \tau_k xC_k$ for all $x > 0$. Thus, by the definition of τ_k there exists a $v > 0$ such that $xC_k \tau_k vC_k$. Since τ is one-one, $v = x$, and τ is therefore also reflexive. τ is therefore a value relation. τ is symmetric, as is shown by the following reasoning. Let $xC_i \tau yC_j$. Since τ is reflexive, $yC_j \tau yC_j$, and thus by the definition of τ_j, $xC_i \tau_j yC_j$. Since τ is complete, there exist $u, v > 0$ such that $uC_j \tau vC_i$; $uC_j \tau uC_j$, and since C_j is a means of circulation, $uC_j \tau_j vC_i$. Since τ_j is homogeneous, it follows that

$$\frac{x}{y}C_i \tau_j 1C_j \text{ and } 1C_j \tau_j \frac{v}{u}C_i.$$

Since τ_j is transitive, $\frac{x}{y}C_i \tau_j \frac{v}{u}C_i$, and since τ_j is one-one, $\frac{x}{y} = \frac{v}{u}$. Since $uC_j \tau vC_i$, it follows from the homogeneity of τ that $yC_j \tau xC_i$. τ is therefore symmetric.

If the money relation induced by a money-commodity C_k coincides with the original interchange relation τ—in other words, if $\tau_k = \tau$—then τ itself must be a transitive value relation and therefore an equivalence relation. (Two relations are equal if for any two quantities of commodities, one relation holds if and only if the other holds.) In general, however, for a given money-commodity C_k it is not the case that $\tau_k = \tau$, even when all commodities are money-commodities. One example of this is the (general) indirect-exchange relation. An equivalent C_k (relative to τ) is called a *uniform equivalent* if the relation induced by C_k coincides with the initial relation, and a money-commodity is called *uniform money-commodity* (relative to τ) if it is a uniform equivalent. An interchange relation τ is said to define a *barter economy*; more concisely, τ itself constitutes barter if τ is a transitive value relation.[4]

The following proposition characterizes barter economies as regards money.

Proposition 4. Let τ be a homogeneous, one-one relation. The following properties of τ are logically equivalent.

(a) τ defines a barter economy.

(b) All commodities are uniform money-commodities.

(c) There is a uniform money-commodity.

(d) All commodities are money-commodities whose money relations coincide.

Demonstration: If (a) is true then τ is a transitive, and hence symmetric, value relation; it follows from the definition of τ_k that $\tau_k = \tau$ for every k. Thus, every commodity is a uniform money-commodity, and (b) is therefore true. (c) follows trivially from (b). If (c) is true, then there is a money commodity C_k such that $\tau_k = \tau$. τ is therefore a transitive value relation and consequently defines a barter economy, so (a) is true. The propositions (a), (b), and (c) are thus equivalent. Since (d) follows trivially from (b), it remains only to demonstrate that (a) follows from (d). Now, if (d) is true, then by proposition 3, τ is a symmetric value relation and $\tau_k = \tau_j$ for some two indices k and j. Now let $xC_i \, \tau \, zC_k$ and $zC_k \, \tau \, yC_j$. Since C_k is a means of circulation, $xC_i \tau_k \, yC_j$. Since $\tau_k = \tau_j$, it follows that $xC_i \, \tau_j \, yC_j$. There thus exists a $v > 0$ such that $xC_i \, \tau \, vC_j$ and $yC_j \, \tau \, vC_j$. Since τ is one-one, it follows that $v = y$, and therefore $xC_i \, \tau \, yC_j$. τ is therefore transitive.

A barter economy is thus characterized by the fact that all commodities are money-commodities and that their money relations coincide (hence the expression 'uniform'). In such an economy a money-commodity is not some specific commodity. This is likewise the case in an economy in which all commodities are money-commodities, which, however, does not necessarily have to be a barter economy. Such an economy is called a *quasi-barter economy* (by Proposition 3 characterized by a symmetric value relation, called quasi-barter for short). It was also shown above that the (general) indirect-exchange relation for a connected matrix E defines a quasi-barter economy, although generally not a barter economy. An economy is designated a money economy if (at least) one commodity plays a special role as a money commodity (relative to τ), but not all commodities are money-commodities. Barter and quasi-barter economies are thus not money-economies. (A pure money economy is a money economy with exactly one money-commodity.)[5]

Although money seems to be a comparatively simple thing, the structures associated with it are quite diverse. A money economy lies between two extremes: one in which no money-commodity exists, the other in which all commodities are money-commodities. A money-commodity may or may not exist, or there may be several. In certain respects (namely, depending on τ, direct or indirect exchange), there may be a money-commodity, and a money-economy exists; in others, there may be no such commodity, and a barter economy exists.

To illustrate this potential variety let us discuss a few simple situations.

As one possibility, let τ be considered direct exchange, (general) indirect exchange, or one-step indirect exchange; in any case it is thus a one-one, homogeneous relation that is also reflexive and symmetric. By Proposition 2, a commodity is a money-commodity (relative to τ) if and only if any quantity of commodities can be expressed through some quantity of this commodity.

The sole trivial situation occurs when there are just two commodities; here a barter economy is the only possibility. Concepts of money are frequently no more than transpositions of this case to situations of many commodities, the result being that the concept is as simple as it is insignificant.[6] In the following figures commodities are represented by points, and direct acts of exchange by connecting lines between them; money commodities are marked by an 'x'; unless otherwise indicated, the propositions refer to the direct-exchange relation.

n = 2:   x ———— x

Figure 11

Fig. 11 represents the case $n = 2$. The subsequent diagrams, for $n = 3$ and $n = 4$, follow on from each other in that one direct exchange drops out each time.

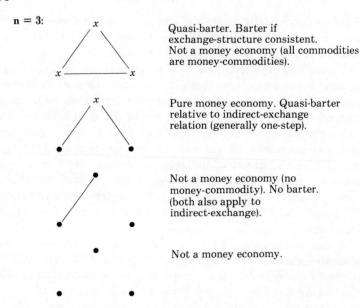

n = 3:

Quasi-barter. Barter if exchange-structure consistent. Not a money economy (all commodities are money-commodities).

Pure money economy. Quasi-barter relative to indirect-exchange relation (generally one-step).

Not a money economy (no money-commodity). No barter. (both also apply to indirect-exchange).

Not a money economy.

Figure 12

The third case corresponds to the example of the weaver–spinner–tailor discussed in chapter 2. (The one-sided use relationships have been deleted here, since they do not facilitate direct exchange). A single money-commodity oriented solely to exchange (whether direct or indirect) cannot provide for the necessary circulation of commodities. The last diagram in fig. 12 is even more extreme. That no acts of direct exchange between the commodities exist, however, does not mean that there are no economic relations between these commodities. A close production relation could well exist between all three commodities; for instance, C_2 is needed to produce C_1, while C_3 is needed to produce C_2, and C_1 is needed to produce C_3. If an arrow indicates the relation of one commodity's being required for the production of another, then this example would appear as in fig. 13 (note the earlier discussion of the use-structure in the case of the weaver, spinner, and tailor).

From the standpoint of production none of the three commodities can be omitted—in Sraffian terms, they are all basic

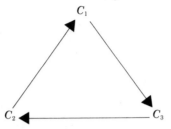

Figure 13

products. Nevertheless, no circulation corresponding to the production-structure is possible here.[7] If circulation takes place by means of money in such circumstances, it will be on the basis of aspects of money not inherent in the money-commodity as discussed so far. In view of such situations, institutional aspects of money, or sociological ones such as 'convention', would have to be introduced.[8]

The duality of the two money-commodities in the second diagram of fig. 14 is of some interest. In a money economy, of course, this duality would be of no importance if there was a symmetrical relationship between the two money-commodities, so that one could be converted into the other at a fixed rate. But this is not to be expected in general, as the quantitative specification depicted in fig. 15 shows. C_1 and C_2 are non-money commodities, while M_1 and M_2 are money-commodities. The numbers indicate how many units of money correspond to each unit of a commodity (τ). Now, let us assume that τ is symmetric, and that $M_1 \, \tau \, aM_2$ holds for a given, yet to be determined uniform exchange rate a. (For example: in two countries, 1 and 2, the same commodities C_1 and C_2 are produced, but through different techniques, which is expressed in the divergent money relations for each of the national currencies M_1 and M_2. A uniform rate of exchange, a, is sought for M_1 and M_2.) As is immediately apparent, there is no number that would allow the conversion from M_1 to M_2 given the money relations between C_1 and C_2. (Values outside the range $\frac{2}{3} \leq a \leq 1$ are in any case excluded from the outset.) The reason is that although two transitive value relations for the commodities C_1 and C_2 can be defined through either M_1 or M_2, as a whole τ is not transitive for any

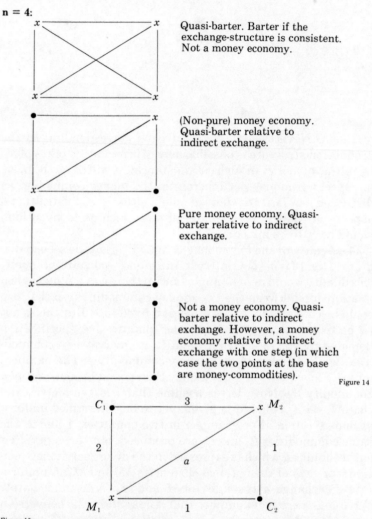

n = 4:

Quasi-barter. Barter if the exchange-structure is consistent. Not a money economy.

(Non-pure) money economy. Quasi-barter relative to indirect exchange.

Pure money economy. Quasi-barter relative to indirect exchange.

Not a money economy. Quasi-barter relative to indirect exchange. However, a money economy relative to indirect exchange with one step (in which case the two points at the base are money-commodities).

Figure 14

Figure 15

value of a. In other words, neither of the money-commodities is a uniform money-commodity. (The figures would suggest that it is more advantageous for country 1 to export C_1 and use M_2 to buy C_2 in country 2, instead of producing C_2 domestically. Likewise for country 2 and C_2. Trade is therefore advantageous, but it could not lead to a single rate of exchange, since there is no mutually acceptable money-commodity, no 'world money' or something similar.)

Despite the variety of possibilities, the general pattern by which commodity circulation occurs in a money economy can be described simply. This pattern will serve as a starting point for subsequent analysis. Let τ be a homogeneous, one-one interchange relation (such as direct-exchange) defining a money economy, and let C_k be a money-commodity (relative to τ). Let E be the (exchange-) matrix corresponding to τ and Z the (circulation-) matrix corresponding to the money-relation τ_k. Then $z_{ij} = \frac{e_{ik}}{e_{jk}} = e_{ik} \cdot e_{kj}$. The proportion e_{ik} expressing one unit of the commodity C_i in terms of the money-commodity, the 'value' of C_i in money, is called the *price* (of a unit) of C_i, and is denoted by p_i. The ratio $z_{ij} = \frac{p_i}{p_j}$ in which two commodities C_i and C_j stand in the money relation is called their *relative price*. Since C_k is a means of circulation, the money relation can be written as follows:

$xC_i \, \tau_k \, yC_j$ if and only if $xC_i \, \tau \, xp_iC_k$ and $yp_jC_k \, \tau \, yC_j$, so that $xp_i = yp_j$, or $\frac{x}{y} = \frac{p_j}{p_i}$.

It can now be stated that circulation proceeds by way of the *sale* of one commodity for money and the *purchase* of another commodity with money. The proportions of the commodities in the money relation are therefore equal to their reciprocal relative price. (The reason for this equality is that for simplicity's sake it was assumed that τ is a homogeneous relation; it need not be the case if homogeneity is not assumed.) Abstractly speaking, the circulation of commodities in a money economy takes place according to the pattern $C-M-C'$; not, however, $C-C'$, which is characteristic of a barter economy (C and C' are two commodities, M a money-commodity). 'Money buys goods and goods buy money; but goods do not buy goods. This restriction is—or ought to be—the central theme of the theory of a money economy.' [9]

2. The Quantity and Circulation of Money

In what follows it is assumed that a money-commodity does exist and that the interchange of commodities occurs by means of the corresponding money relation, which is thus a transitive value relation. Let a monetary unit U be established for the money-commodity. The interchange of commodities consists in a quantity of a commodity being sold for a sum of money, and in another act, a quantity of a commodity being bought with a sum of money (as in the discussion above). Let us now focus on those aspects of these operations that concern the *transaction* of money itself, leaving aside the underlying exchange of commodities between owners. Instead of considering the whole gamut of commodities, then, we shall concentrate on just one, the money-commodity, the quantity of which, its greater or lesser availability, is an important magnitude. The circulation of commodities requires not merely the existence of a money-commodity, but also enough of it to allow commerce. The quantity of money has thus long played an important role in political economy, indeed a very controversial one even today. In contrast to the various traditional formulations of a quantity theory and a so-called quantity equation of money,[10] this study will consider not only the sheer quantity of money but also its structural aspects: the *transaction-structure* between the owners of commodities, which specifies who has to pay how much to whom; and the *localization* of the total quantity of money, which specifies how many monetary units the individual commodity-owners possess.

Let $A_1, \ldots, A_n$ represent the individual owners of commodities. In accordance with the procedure of chapter 1, let y_i be the quantity of commodity C_i held by A_i and y_{ij} the quantity of C_i that the owner A_j of C_j wishes to acquire. In short

$$A_i \xrightarrow{\;y_{ij}\;} A_j \text{ such that } y_i = \sum_{j=1}^{n} y_{ij}.$$

Since we will now consider only the relationship between the A_i, we may assume that $y_{ii} = 0$ for every i. If p_i is the price of a unit of C_i, then the sum of money A_j must pay A_i to acquire y_{ij} is x_{ji}

$= y_{ij} \cdot p_i$. Instead of the use-relationship $A_i \xrightarrow{\text{commodity}} A_j$, we will henceforth consider the money-transaction it induces, namely $A_i \xleftarrow{\text{money}} A_j$, which runs in the direction opposite to that in which commodities change hands. The transaction-structure among the $A_1, \ldots, A_n$ is thus defined by $n(n-1)$ elementary acts of the form

$$A_i \xrightarrow{\quad x_{ij} \quad} A_j \quad i, j = 1, \ldots, n, \text{ where } i \neq j.$$

The arrow indicates who has to pay whom, the x_{ij} the amount of payment in U. This structure is based on the assumption that A_i has to pay for the whole consignment at once; delivery in stages or on credit is thus excluded so as not to complicate the central issue with extraneous matters. Since a commodity-owner who enters into no transaction with *any* other commodity-owner is irrelevant, such individuals are excluded from consideration.

The following then applies for the *transaction matrix X* of the payments x_{ij}: for $i \neq j$, $x_{ij} > 0$ or $x_{ij} = 0$ (in the latter case the corresponding arrow may be dropped from the diagram). Moreover, $x_{ii} = 0$ for every i, and for every i there exists a j such that $x_{ij} > 0$ or $x_{ji} > 0$. This characteristic applies to any connected matrix X, although conversely, a transaction matrix is not necessarily connected. (For example: if X has only one positive column.) The total value of all transactions (in U) is given by N

$$= \sum_{i, j = 1}^{n} x_{ij},$$ the *transaction value*. It is connected to the use-

structure by $N = \sum\limits_{j, i = 1}^{n} y_{ji} p_j = \sum\limits_{j = 1}^{n} y_j p_j = y \cdot p$, where y is the

vector of the y_i ($y \cdot p$ is the dot product of two vectors). Since y specifies the total amount of every commodity traded in the transactions between owners, y can also be called the *transaction volume*, though it should be noted that y is not a quantity but a vector. (The prefix 'transaction' will be dropped whenever no loss of meaning is possible.) The transaction-structure X mirrors the structure of use and exchange of commodities, but since money is a very general expression of the relations among commodities, use and exchange cannot generally be read off the transaction-structure.

60

Now to the crucial question: what total quantity of money M must be available for all transactions to be able to proceed, and how is this quantity connected to the transaction-structure and the money holdings of individual commodity-owners? (And what is its relationship to the volume of transactions and prices?) The money holdings of A_i are given by a vector x whose components x_i (with $x_i > 0$ or $x_i = 0$) specify the holdings. Since the sum total of money M is composed of the money holdings of all the A_i—in other words, $M = \sum_{i=1}^{n} x_i$— the vector x can also be called a *localization* of M. A simple example in which $n = 3$ will illustrate the basic concept. The transaction-structure, consisting of $3(3-1) = 6$ elementary acts, has the configuration illustrated in fig. 16.

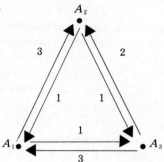

Figure 16

The transaction-value is $N = 11$ (all subsequent numbers are quantities of U). It is immediately apparent that a sum of money $M = 11$ suffices for all transactions to proceed; the localization is $x = (4, 2, 5)$ (i.e. $x_1 = 4$, $x_2 = 2$, $x_3 = 5$). But a money total $M = 6$ would also suffice, as shown by fig. 17, which depicts the flow of the sum of money among the commodity-owners under a localization $x = (3, 0, 3)$.

The circled numbers in fig. 17 specify the localization, the dotted lines the connections between income and outgo for each A_i; the diagram as a whole represents the flow of sums of money among the owners; sums not involved in transactions are not shown. As can be seen, in this flow 1 unit (U) is involved in 4 transactions, $1U$ in 3 transactions, and $4U$ in 1 transaction.

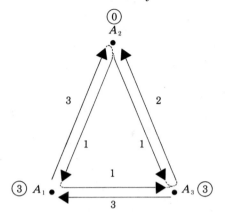

Figure 17

A sum of money $M = 3$ would even suffice, as shown by fig. 18, illustrating the flow for a localization $x = (0, 0, 3)$. In this situation $1U$ is involved in 5 transactions, $1U$ in 4, and $1U$ in 2.

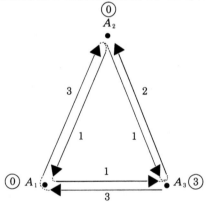

Figure 18

A moment's thought shows that a sum smaller than $M = 3$ would not suffice for all transactions, whatever localization was selected. Hence, $3U$ is the minimum sum of money required for this transaction-structure. It is also evident that the question of whether or not a particular sum of money is sufficient depends on the localization. For example, a localization $x = (1, 0, 2)$ of the minimum sum $M = 3$ would not be sufficient to effect all transactions.

This example demonstrates that the question of whether or not a sum of money M is sufficient to effect transactions of a total value N is closely linked both to the localization of this sum of money among the individual owners and to the flow, in particular the number of transactions in which the monetary-units are involved. It also shows that the total value N is not the only relevant factor; the transaction-structure X must be taken into account too.

This interconnection may now be formulated for the general situation. (The example above will come up again later.) Let X be a transaction-structure of value $N = \sum_{i,j=1}^{n} x_{ij}$, and let M be a sum of money circulating in this transaction-structure to allow the interchange of commodities (the sum may not necessarily be sufficient). Further, let x be a localization of M, so that $M = \sum_{i=1}^{n} x_i$. Now let there be a given circulation of M, and let s denote the number of transactions in which a unit of money can be involved. s can assume values between 1 and $n(n-1)$. For any given s, let m_s denote the number of units of M involved in that number of transactions. Then

$$M = \sum_{s=1}^{n(n-1)} m_s \text{ and}$$

$$S = \sum_{s=1}^{n(n-1)} m_s \cdot s \text{ is called the } transaction \; sum \text{ of } M.$$

$$v = \frac{S}{M} = \sum_{s=1}^{n(n-1)} \frac{m_s}{M} \cdot s \text{ is called the } mean \; transaction \; number,$$

or the average 'velocity' of circulation of a unit of the sum of money M in circulation. The transaction sum depends on the sum of money M, its localization, the observed circulation (characterized by the numbers m_s), and the transaction-structure. The same sum of money can yield differing transaction sums if these variables change. The dependence of the transaction sum (with a given transaction-structure and circulation) on the localization is denoted by $S = S(x)$.

The mean transaction number is a weighted average of all transaction numbers and can assume values between 1 and $n(n-1)$.

A sum of money M may now be said to be *sufficient* under a given localization x if a circulation exists such that $S(x) = N$. M is therefore sufficient if and only if under a suitable distribution of M among the individual commodity-owners, all transactions, of total value N, can be effected with M. The above example shows that several different sums of money may suffice, but not every sum will do so. There is always some sufficient sum of money; for example, $M = N$, under a localization $x_i = \sum\limits_{j=1}^{n} x_{ij}$ and a circulation such that $m_1 = N$ and $m_s = 0$ for $s \geq 2$, is always a sufficient sum of money; v would then equal 1. Any satisfactorily large sum of money M—or more precisely, $M \geq N$—is therefore sufficient. Accordingly, there will be a smallest possible sufficient sum of money $\overline{M}$, which is of special interest. $\overline{M}$ is defined as $\overline{M} = \min\{ \sum\limits_{i=1}^{n} x_i \mid S(x) = N \}$ and is called the *minimum sum of money*. Since N and all larger sums of money are trivially sufficient, the relevant sufficient sums lie between $\overline{M}$ and N. For $\overline{M}$ itself the following simple *inequality* holds under any transaction-structure:

$$\frac{N}{n(n-1)} \leq \max_{i,\,j\,=\,1,\,2,\,\ldots,\,n} x_{ij} \leq \overline{M} \leq N$$

Demonstration. Trivially $\overline{M} \leq N$, and since no elementary transaction can be effected in stages, $\overline{M}$ must be at least as large as the largest individual transaction value. And $N = \sum\limits_{i,\,j\,=\,1}^{n} x_{ij} \leq \max\limits_{i,\,j} x_{ij} \cdot n(n-1)$ (the diagonal of X is zero).

The following two examples show that the minimum sum of money can actually assume the limiting values of this inequality under certain transaction-structures, which means that a sum of money smaller than the total transaction value is sometimes not sufficient, but that a sum of money corresponding to the largest value of the individual transactions may be sufficient to effect all transactions.

Examples

As is easily seen, in the following transaction-structure, the flow of money is blocked such that each unit of money can be involved in only one transaction, and $\overline{M} = N$:

$$A_1 \xrightarrow{x_{12}} A_2 \xleftarrow{x_{32}} A_3 \xrightarrow{x_{34}} A_4 \xleftarrow{x_{54}} \ldots A_n.$$

The opposite is the case for the transaction-structure generated by the following elementary acts:

$$A_i \underset{m}{\overset{m}{\longleftarrow}} A_j \text{ for all } i, j = 1, \ldots, n, i \neq j,$$

where m is a particular amount of money. Clearly, in this structure there is a possible circulation of the sum of money such that each unit of m is used in all transactions. Hence $v = n(n-1)$, and it follows that $\dfrac{N}{n(n-1)} = \max_{i,j} x_{ij} = m$ is the minimum sum of money.

An example that lies between these extremes and also illustrates some of the general concepts is the transaction-structure of the use-structure in the case of the weaver, spinner, and tailor discussed in chapter 2 (except that we now assume a circulation of commodities involving money). Fig. 19 depicts the situation.

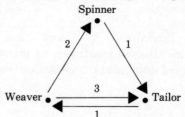

Figure 19

Here $N = 7$, $\dfrac{N}{n(n-1)} \dfrac{7}{6}$, $\max_{i,j} x_{ij} = 3$, and the minimum sum of money is thus $\overline{M} = 4$, under the only possible localization, namely that the weaver holds the entire sum of money (in general there will be several possible localizations for the minimum sum of money). The corresponding maximum mean transaction number is $\bar{v} = \frac{7}{4}$. In this case, the inequality for a minimum sum of money is a strict inequality throughout:

$$\frac{N}{n(n-1)} < \max_{i,j} x_{ij} < \overline{M} < N.$$

The following proposition follows from the dependence of the transaction sum of a particular sum of money on the localization of that sum of money and the transaction-structure: if a sum is sufficient and the localization and/or the transaction-structure alters, then an alteration of the sum of money is required if all transactions are to be effected. (This applies in particular to the minimum sum of money. Other examples could be designed to illustrate the point.) In this context, the sought-after quantity equation for money can be critically described: *if* M is a sufficient sum of money (given a particular transaction-structure and suitable localization), then $S = N$, and hence $N = v \cdot M$. Since N is linked to the quantities of commodities through the equation $N = y \cdot p$, it follows that $y \cdot p = M \cdot v$ (relative to a given transaction-structure and a localization), the *quantity equation for money*. This equation often arises purely by definition, in which case it is a tautology. But that is not the case here, since the two sides of the equation have mutually independent meanings. The components of the left side, the vectors y and p, are defined independently of those of the right side, and the definition of v relates *solely* to M and S, and not to the transaction value $N = y \cdot p$. The equation states that a sum of money M with a mean transaction number v (which depends in general on the transaction-structure and in particular on the localization of M) is sufficient to effect transactions of a given (total) transaction value. This may or may not be the case, and as we have already seen, with the same sum of money M it may be true for one transaction-structure with a given localization, but not for others. (The operative definition here is that of v as $\frac{S}{M}$, in which neither y nor p plays any role.)

In subsequent discussion, the connection expressed in the quantity equation between y and p on one side and M and v on the other will be adopted as a basis, *if* the sum of money is sufficient. This connection will often be used to establish a relationship between the sum of money and prices and, when exchange-ratios are fixed, between the sum of money and the level of prices. Some relationship, of course, does exist—namely the quantity equation (when the sum of money is sufficient)— but a closer, more causal one is meant here: an increase in M leads to a proportional increase in all prices. The core of this connection can be formulated as follows: a doubling (or halving) of the sum of money entails a doubling (or halving) of prices.[11] The first example above, in which $n = 3$, can be taken to test this proposition. Let us examine two situations in which the sum of money is halved.

Situation 1. Halving the sum of money while the transaction-structure remains unchanged but the localization alters. Let $M = 6$ and $x = (3, 0, 3)$, a localization of M. The flow for this structure is thus: $m_1 = 4$, $m_3 = 1$, $m_4 = 1$, and otherwise $m_s = 0$. Hence $S = 4 \cdot 1 + 1 \cdot 3 + 1 \cdot 4 = 11 = N$, and $M = 6$ is therefore a sufficient sum of money. $v = \dfrac{S}{M} = \dfrac{11}{6}$. Now let the sum of money be reduced by half, to $M = 3$, with a different localization $x = (0, 0, 3)$. This case was also considered above: the relevant flow is $m_1 = 1$, $m_4 = 1$, $m_5 = 1$ and otherwise $m_s = 0$. Hence $S = 1 \cdot 2 + 1 \cdot 4 + 1 \cdot 5 = 11 = N$, and $M = 3$ is therefore a sufficient sum of money. $v = \dfrac{S}{M} = \dfrac{11}{3}$.

Thus, the halving of the sum of money doubled the mean transaction number with no necessary change in price, let alone a reduction by half.

Situation 2. Now let us imagine that the sum of money is halved under a constant localization but altered transaction-structure. We will make just one change in the transaction-structure, altering the quantities of the transaction matrix such that none of the arrows disappear and no new ones emerge; the +, 0-structure of the matrix, the real structure of interconnections, will not change. Let $M = 6$, with localization $x = (2, 0, 4)$. It is immediately apparent, as in situation 1, that M is a sufficient sum of money, and that $v = \dfrac{S}{M} = \dfrac{11}{6}$. Now let the sum of money be halved while the localization remains the same. As indicated previously, $M = 3$ is not sufficient under this localization. If the sum of money is halved, then all transactions can no longer be effected; there exists no mean transaction number v for $M = 3$ such that the quantity equation can be met for the original transactions. The transaction-structure thus has to change—through a shift in the volume of transactions y, the prices p, or both—if the sum of money of $3U$ under the localization $\frac{x}{2} = (1, 0, 2)$ is to suffice. One possible change, with its corresponding flow, is illustrated in fig. 20. All payments remain the same, except that from A_3 to A_2 which falls

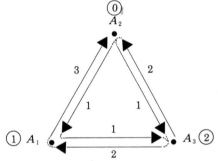

Figure 20

from $3U$ to $2U$. The total transaction value thus falls to $N = 10$. The mean transaction number rises from $\frac{11}{6}$ to $\frac{10}{3}$. Since the halving of M increases v, not all prices can be halved (if the transaction volume remains constant). Moreover: the ratio $\frac{x_{13}}{x_{31}}$ of transaction values between A_1 and A_3 rises by a factor of $\frac{3}{2}$. Thus, if the quantitative ratio of deliveries between A_1 and A_3 remains the same, then the relative prices of C_3 and C_1 must change. Moreover, it can be seen that not all quantitative ratios between owners can remain unchanged. Hence: a reduction of the sum of money by half has augmented the mean transaction number; a halving of all prices is not possible (with a constant transaction volume), and in general relative prices will change.

Taken together, these examples show that a halving of the sum of money will not necessarily bring about a halving of prices. Indeed, prices can remain constant (if the localization changes), or shift unevenly (if the transaction-structure changes). It is formally correct that *if* the mean transaction number remains unchanged and the halved sum of money still suffices to effect all the original transactions, then the level of prices will be halved. But this would be a crude view of the matter, for it ignores the intricate connections among transaction-structure, localization, and sum of money. As I have sought to demonstrate, the causal connections of the sum of money are far more complicated. In particular, a variation in the sum of money should not be expected to leave the mean transaction number constant.

Since the analysis of the interconnection expressed in the quantity equation can become quite complex, it is advisable to abandon this equality in favour of the inequality involving the minimum sum of money, which is valid for any transaction-structure, regardless of localization. This inequality also draws attention to a lack of symmetry in the relationship between prices and the sum of money: if M is a sufficient sum of money for a given transaction-structure, then $\overline{M} \leq M$. The minimum sum of money $\overline{M}$ and its corresponding maximum mean transaction number $\overline{v}$ are characteristic magnitudes of the transaction-structure, which yield an estimation of M from below:

$$\frac{1}{n(n-1)} \, (p \cdot y) \leq \frac{1}{\overline{v}} \, (p \cdot y) \leq M$$

(in which the second inequality is independent even of the transaction-structure).

It is therefore plausible that an expansion of production or a rise in the level of prices will eventually require an expansion of the sum of money (since credit has been excluded here). Less plausible is the converse conclusion, that an expansion of the sum of money (even beyond N) will eventually lead to an extension of production or a rise in prices. But such considerations acquire substance only if money is considered as a store of value and credit is brought into the analysis.

The results of this chapter, developed in response to the question posed at its beginning, may now be summarized.

Results

1.   A money-commodity serves to place all other commodities in a transitive value relation with one another, the money-relation. It is not necessary that a money-commodity exist, but on the other hand several may exist. The money-relation between commodities does not necessarily coincide with the direct- and indirect-exchange relations that rest on the use-structure. Moreover, it may happen (even under connected production-structures) that no money relation is possible on the basis of exchange alone.

2.   If a money-commodity exists, then all commodities have a price. The relative price of two commodities is the proportion in which they stand in the money relation. In a money economy— one in which money plays a special role—the circulation of commodities proceeds not through the exchange of commodities for one another, but through the sale of commodities for money and the purchase of commodities with money, in accordance, of course, with their relative price.

3.   As a means of circulation, the money-commodity must be available in a certain quantity and owned by individuals. Whether or not a particular sum of money suffices to effect all transactions depends not only on the volume of transactions and their structure but also on the localization of the sum of money among the commodity-owners. The connection between commodity prices and the sum of money, expressed in the quantity equation (in its non-tautological version), thus depends on the transaction-structure and the localization and in general is not proportional.

4
Concrete Labour and Use-Structure

So far production itself has not been closely examined. To rectify this, let us recall the diagrams of production presented in chapter 1, in which products are depicted as the outcome of different types of labour in conjunction with means of production. To ascertain the total labour a society requires to manufacture a product, both the direct labour expended on that product and the concrete acts of labour that contributed indirectly through manufacture of the corresponding means of production must be considered. This chapter will be devoted to answering the following basic question. What concrete labours, and in what proportions, are required to produce a given unit of some commodity, and how do these expenditures of labour depend on the use-structure (and in particular on the division into means of production and of consumption)?

Let us begin with the following, highly stylized example.

The example of coal and iron.   Two products, coal and iron, are manufactured through labour, and both are required as means of production both in their own production and in the production of the other. More precisely, the mining of coal requires iron in the shape of instruments of labour, and coal is needed as an energy source to operate these tools; labour is required in the concrete form of mining-labour. The production of iron in an iron-smelter requires iron in the shape of the instruments of labour, and coal is likewise needed to operate these tools; labour is required in the concrete form of smelting-labour. Both coal and iron are therefore means of production.

The *production-structure* for the two products can then be expressed as follows, in accordance with the formulation in chapter 1. Let C_1 represent 1 tonne of coal, C_2 1 tonne of iron; let *M*-labour represent 1 hour of mining-labour and *S*-labour represent 1 hour of smelting-labour.

Then:

Mining: $(2\ M\text{-labour}, \frac{1}{2}\ C_1, \frac{1}{5}\ C_2) \rightarrow C_1$

Smelting: $(3\ S\text{-labour}, \frac{1}{4}\ C_1, \frac{1}{2}\ C_2) \rightarrow C_2$

If we deduct from the total output the amount of each product required for its own production, we obtain the *net output*:

Mining: $(2\ M\text{-labour}, \frac{1}{5}\ C_2) \rightarrow \frac{1}{2}\ C_1$

Smelting: $(3\ S\text{-labour}, \frac{1}{4}\ C_1) \rightarrow \frac{1}{2}\ C_2.$

We are assuming *constant returns to scale*: a given multiplication of inputs results in a corresponding multiplication of output. The social interconnection between the two branches of production then means that

For coal: $(2\ M\text{-labour}, (\frac{6}{5}\ S\text{-labour}, \frac{1}{10}\ C_1)) \rightarrow \frac{1}{2}\ C_1$

For iron: $(3\ S\text{-labour}, (1\ M\text{-labour}, \frac{1}{10}\ C_2)) \rightarrow \frac{1}{2}\ C_2.$

The net output is

Coal: $(2\ M\text{-labour}, \frac{6}{5}\ S\text{-labour}) \rightarrow \frac{2}{5}\ C_1$

Iron: $(3\ S\text{-labour}, 1\ M\text{-labour}) \rightarrow \frac{2}{5}\ C_2,$

and finally, assuming constant returns to scale,

Coal: $(5\ M\text{-labour}, 3\ S\text{-labour}) \rightarrow C_1$

Iron: $(2.5\ M\text{-labour}, 7.5\ S\text{-labour}) \rightarrow C_2.$

From the standpoint of society as a whole, then, both concrete labours are required for the production of coal and iron, in particular amounts given by the production-structure. In other words, through the production-structure both products can be represented as the results of labour alone—indeed of distinct concrete labours. This presentation has the character of an aggregate social balance-sheet; in contrast to the (highly stylized) production-structure, it is not a technical relation.

It might now seem tempting to compare coal and iron in terms of the varying amounts of labour required to produce them. But this is not possible, since coal requires more mining-labour but less smelting-labour than iron. If the two expenditures of labour are to be compared, an hour of mining-labour must be set equivalent to some number of hours of smelting-labour—but by what criterion? (The next chapter will discuss the mechanism of an equating in the form of commodity exchange.)

The general case of the production relations of two products can be depicted analogously to the coal-iron example:

$$(l_1 \text{ type 1}, a_{11} C_1, a_{21} C_2) \rightarrow C_1$$

$$(l_2 \text{ type 2}, a_{12} C_1, a_{22} C_2) \rightarrow C_2$$

In terms of expenditure of labour of type 1 and type 2:

$$(\frac{(1-a_{22}) l_1}{D} \text{ type 1}, \frac{a_{21} l_2}{D} \text{ type 2}) \rightarrow C_1$$

$$(\frac{a_{12} l_1}{D} \text{ type 1}, \frac{(1-a_{11}) l_2}{D} \text{ type 2}) \rightarrow C_2$$

in which $D = (1-a_{11})(1-a_{22}) - a_{12} a_{21}$.

This representation of the products in terms of labour alone emerges unambiguously from the production-structure. Labour of type 2 (in addition to direct labour of type 1) enters into the representation of C_1 if and only if $a_{21} > 0$; in other words, if C_2 is really used in the production of C_1 (and analogously for C_2; $l_i > 0$ for every i). Indeed, this representation is meaningful only if

$$a_{11} < 1, \, a_{22} < 1, \, a_{12} a_{21} < (1-a_{11})(1-a_{22}).$$

(This is called the Hawkins-Simon condition.) If these requirements are not met, some expenditures of labour are infinite or negative.

What do these requirements mean? The condition that $a_{11} < 1$ and $a_{22} < 1$ is immediately evident, since otherwise labour would have to be added to one unit of product in order to manufacture (at least) one unit of the same product—and that, of course, would be a process of destruction instead of production. In the following example these two conditions are met, but not $a_{12}a_{21} < (1-a_{11})(1-a_{22})$:

$$(1 \text{ type } 1, \frac{4}{5}C_2) \rightarrow C_1$$

$$(1 \text{ type } 2, \frac{3}{2}C_1) \rightarrow C_2.$$

Here each individual production process makes sense on its own, but the two together do not, since from the standpoint of society as a whole, we have (as in the coal-iron example):

$$(1 \text{ type } 1, \frac{4}{5} \text{ type } 2, \frac{6}{5}C_1) \rightarrow C_1$$

$$(1 \text{ type } 2, \frac{3}{2} \text{ type } 1, \frac{6}{5}C_2) \rightarrow C_2.$$

In society as a whole, not only does the input of labour fail to produce any more than already existed, but a portion of the inputs $(\frac{1}{5}C_1, \frac{1}{5}C_2)$ are actually destroyed. (And the expenditures of labour for both products are correspondingly negative.) In other words, the production-structure is *unproductive from the standpoint of society as a whole.*[1]

This state of affairs can also be depicted in a manner that will give us a hint about the general situation involving n commodities. Assume that x_1 units of C_1 and x_2 units of C_2 are manufactured. In the example above, then, the amount of C_2 used in production is $\frac{4}{5}x_1$, while $\frac{3}{2}x_2$ of C_1 is used. For the system to be productive (that is, for more of each product to be produced than is used up), it must be the case that $\frac{3}{2}x_2 < x_1$ and $\frac{4}{5}x_1 < x_2$. But this condition cannot be fulfilled for any pair $x = (x_1, x_2)$ of non-negative numbers. If A is the matrix of the a_{ij} (see chapter 1), which would mean in this example

$$A = \begin{pmatrix} 0 & \frac{3}{2} \\ \frac{4}{5} & 0 \end{pmatrix}, \text{ then this}$$

requirement may also be written: $A \cdot x < x$. In general, a production-structure corresponding to the production of n commodities

74

—or alternatively, the $n \times n$ matrix A that represents this structure—will be termed *productive* if there exists a vector x of activities $x_i \geq 0$ for $i = 1, 2, \ldots, n$, such that $A \cdot x < x$. This may be written: $\sum\limits_{j=1}^{n} a_{ij}x_j < x_i$ for $i = 1, 2, \ldots, n$.

In words: A production-*structure* is termed productive if, under a given activation of the production processes, the amount of product consumed is less than the amount produced, for every product. For the special case $n = 2$, A is productive if and only if the Hawkins-Simon conditions are fulfilled: $a_{11} < 1$, $a_{22} < 1$, $a_{12}a_{21} < (1-a_{11})(1-a_{22})$. (See the mathematical appendix, part 1.)

Having examined these examples, let us now consider the *general case of the production of n commodities*, with an $n \times n$ production matrix A and an n-vector of direct expenditures of labour $l > 0$. We will denote the diagonal matrix diag l by L. By applying the successive procedure used in the coal-iron example, we may obtain a representation of the n commodities in terms of concrete labour alone. But we will formulate this procedure—based on constant returns to scale, the interconnection of production, and the net output—more simply.[2]

Proposition 1. For every $j = 1, 2, \ldots, n$, there exist non-negative coefficients $v_{1j}, v_{2j}, \ldots v_{nj}$ such that

$$(v_{1j}l_1 \text{ type } 1, v_{2j}l_2 \text{ type } 2, \ldots, v_{nj}l_n \text{ type } n) \rightarrow C_j$$

The $n \times n$ matrix V of the v_{ij} is given by $V = (I-A)^{-1}$.

Demonstration. Let $x = (x_1, \ldots, x_n)$ be a vector of non-negative activities; then the processes $(l_j, a_{1j}, a_{2j}, \ldots, a_{nj}) \rightarrow 1C_j$ $(j = 1, \ldots, n)$, multiplied by the x_j and collected according to different inputs of the same commodity for the system as a whole, yield

$$(Lx, Ax) \rightarrow x.$$

x thus represents the vector of the output of production, Ax the corresponding vector of expenditures of means of production, and Lx the corresponding vector of expenditures of labour of various types. Constant returns to scale and the interconnection of production are assumed. The net output is then

$$Lx \rightarrow x - Ax.$$

The vector $y = x - Ax$ of net product is thus produced by means of Lx expenditures of labour. Since A is productive, the Leontief inverse $V = (I-A)^{-1}$ exists, and $V \geq 0$ (see mathematical appendix, part 1, Proposition 1). Hence $x = (I-A)^{-1}y = Vy$. The net output is therefore

$$LVy \rightarrow y$$

for every non-negative vector y of net products. That the system generates exactly one unit of C_j as net product corresponds to the special case in which $y = t_j$, where t_j is an n-vector whose jth component is 1 and all of whose other components are 0. Since $LVt_j = (l_1 v_{1j}, l_2 v_{2j}, \ldots, l_n v_{nj})$, manufacture of an additional unit of C_j requires an expenditure of labours of different types: $(v_{1j} l_1$ type $1, \ldots, v_{nj} l_n$ type $n)$.

As a rule, not all concrete labours are indirectly required to produce a unit of a particular commodity. In other words, for some i in the formulation of Proposition 1, $v_{ij} = 0$.

Proposition 2.   For every $j = 1, \ldots, n$, $v_{jj} > 0$. For $i \neq j$, $v_{ij} > 0$ if and only if C_i enters directly or indirectly into the production of C_j.

Demonstration.   That C_i enters directly or indirectly into the production of C_j means that there is a chain from i to j through production (see chapter 2, section 2). Proposition 2 thus follows from part 1 of the mathematical appendix (Proposition 2).

The following conclusion follows from part 1 of the mathematical appendix (corollary to Proposition 2 and note 2 to Proposition 1): All concrete labours are indirectly required to produce a unit of every commodity if and only if A is connected; for every commodity, no indirect concrete labours in addition to the direct labour are required if and only if A is a diagonal matrix.

Connected and diagonal production-structures thus constitute limiting cases: in the first, production is strongly interlinked, in the second not at all. Since some interconnection generally exists, some concrete labours will appear in the representation of a commodity as in Proposition 1, but not all, unless the interconnection is extremely pronounced (and the matrix connected).

One simple classification of commodities according to interconnection is the division between means of production and means of consumption. Let $C_1, \ldots, C_p$, $p \leq n$, be the commodities used as means of production (even if not necessarily exclusively), and $C_{p+1}, \ldots, C_n$ be the commodities used exclusively for consumption; these will be of less importance in the examination of production.

The production relations then have the form

$$(l_j, a_{ij}, \ldots, a_{pj}) \to C_j \text{ for } 1 \leq j \leq n$$

since by definition $a_{ij} = 0$, when $i \geq p + 1$. Let A^* be the $p \times p$ matrix of the a_{ij} for $1 \leq i, j \leq p$, and let A_* be the $p \times (n-p)$ matrix of the a_{ij} for $1 \leq i \leq p, p + 1 \leq j \leq n$. A^* describes the production of means of production by means of these means of production, and A_* the production of means of consumption by means of the means of production. The overall production-structure then has the form:

$$A = \begin{pmatrix} A^* & A_* \\ 0 & 0 \end{pmatrix}.$$

If V^* and V_* are defined analogously with A^* and A_* (with the v_{ij} instead of the a_{ij}), then

Proposition 3.

$$V = \begin{pmatrix} V^* & V_* \\ 0 & I \end{pmatrix} \text{ and}$$

$$V^* = (I-A^*)^{-1}$$
$$V_* = (I-A^*)^{-1}A_*$$

Demonstration. V has the form $V = \begin{pmatrix} V^* & V_* \\ R & S \end{pmatrix}$ with

appropriate matrices R and S. Since $I = V(I-A)$, it follows that

$$I = \begin{pmatrix} V^* & V_* \\ R & S \end{pmatrix} \cdot \begin{pmatrix} I-A^* & -A_* \\ O & I \end{pmatrix} = \begin{pmatrix} V^*(I-A^*)-V^*A_*+V_* \\ R(I-A^*) & -RA_* + S \end{pmatrix}$$

hence $V^*(I-A^*) = I, -V^*A_* + V_* = 0, R(I-A^*) = 0, -RA_* + S = I$. ($O$ and I are the null-matrix and identity matrix of the appropriate dimension.) Since A is productive, so is A^*, and the Leontief inverse $(I-A^*)^{-1}$ consequently exists. (See mathematical appendix, part 1.) Hence $V^* = (I-A^*)^{-1}$, $V_* = V^*A_* = (I-A^*)^{-1}A_*$. It then follows that $R = O$, and consequently $S = I$.

Propositions 1 and 3 provide the grounds for:

Conclusion. In the representation of a means of production (as in Proposition 1), the only types of labour that enter in are those directly required to produce means of production; the coefficients v_{ij} that thus arise are determined solely by the production-structure A^* of the means of production. In the representation of a means of consumption (as in Proposition 1), the only types of labour that enter in, apart from that directly required for its production, are those directly required for the production of means of production; the coefficients v_{ij} that thus arise depend both on the production-structure A^* of means of production and on the production-structure A_* of means of consumption.

To illustrate these propositions, let us look again at the coal-iron example.

$$A = \begin{pmatrix} \dfrac{1}{2} & \dfrac{1}{4} \\ \dfrac{1}{5} & \dfrac{1}{2} \end{pmatrix}, l = \begin{pmatrix} 2 \\ 3 \end{pmatrix}$$

A is connected, $A^* = A$.

$$V = (I-A)^{-1} = \begin{pmatrix} \dfrac{5}{2} & \dfrac{5}{4} \\ 1 & \dfrac{5}{2} \end{pmatrix}.$$

Proposition 1 yields the initially specified expenditures of labour for iron and coal.

The principal results of this chapter may be summarized as follows.[3]

1. If the production-structure is productive, then any product can be depicted as the outcome of labour alone:

$$(v_{1j} l_1 \text{ type } 1, \dots, v_{nj} l_n \text{ type } n) \to C_j$$

This expression indicates the expenditures of labour of different types required by society as a whole to produce a given unit of a commodity.

2. The non-negative coefficients v_{ij} are given unambiguously through the production-structure. Which concrete labours actually turn up (i.e., with a positive value) in any given expression depends on the interconnections of the production-structure, and in particular on which commodities are means of production and which are means of consumption.

5
Abstract Labour and the Money Relation

So far we have examined two sides of a market economy, each separately: the 'visible' side of circulation, particularly the value-form and the money relation; and production, in the 'invisible' shape of the aggregate social expenditure of differing types of labour. The specific connection of these two aspects must now be analysed. The basic question is this: What is the significance of the value-form, and in particular the money relation, of the products of labour for the various concrete labours themselves?

We will seek the answer through an analytic concept of 'abstract' labour. The following passage offers a useful point of reference, and also makes clear its contrast to various other notions of abstract labour.[1]

'Men do not therefore bring the products of their labour into relation with each other as values because they see (*gelten*) these objects merely as the material integuments of homogeneous (*gleichartig*) human labour. The reverse is true: by equating (*gleichsetzen*) their different products to each other in exchange as values, they equate their different kinds of labour as human labour. They do this without being aware of it.'

Granted, this formulation is still very rough and imprecise, as is shown by the use of such terms as *gleichartig* (literally, 'of the same kind'), *gelten* ('counts as'), and *gleichsetzen*. But the basic idea can be symbolized as in fig. 21.

The phrase 'the reverse is true' can be expressed this way: the money relation induces a particular relation for the concrete labours themselves, called 'abstract labour'. The derivation of

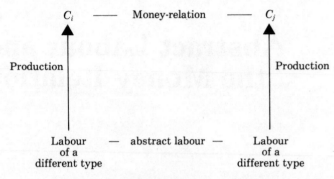

C_i ——— Money-relation ——— C_j

Production   Production

Labour — abstract labour — Labour
of a   of a
different type   different type

Figure 21

this relation will provide the essential answer to the first part of the basic question. The answer to the second part lies in the fact that, because of the character of labour as abstract labour, the exchange ratios between commodities are subject to certain limitations, and their connection becomes closer.

1. Abstract Labour: a Simple Example

To begin with, let us demonstrate the construction of the concept of abstract labour through the simple coal-iron example described in chapter 4. The amounts of differing concrete labour expended to produce coal and iron were as follows.

Coal (C_1):   (5 M-labour, 3 S-labour) $\rightarrow C_1$
Iron (C_2):   (2.5 M-labour, 7.5 S-labour) $\rightarrow C_2$.

In the framework of an exchange relation τ alone (direct exchange, for example), without considering these expenditures of labour, the ratio of coal and iron is fairly arbitrary, there being no reason for any particular exchange ratio. From the standpoint of production, however, coal and iron represent two quite determinate complexes of concrete labours, namely $x = $ (5 M-labour, 3 S-labour) and $y = $ (2.5 M-labour, 7.5 S-labour. In other words, they are two uniquely determined points in the 'space of concrete labours' $\Re_+^2$ spanned by the two concrete labours mining and smelting. For a diagrammatic representation , see fig. 22.

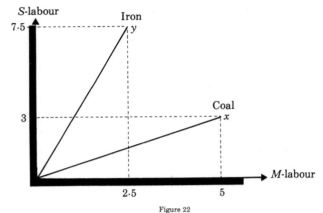

Figure 22

The two complexes x and y are linearly independent.

Now let C_k be a money-commodity and τ_k the corresponding money relation. C_k can be a produced commodity (even C_1 or C_2), but this is not necessary; it is sufficient that the relation τ be defined for C_k and that C_k be a money-commodity relative to τ. Since τ_k is a transitive value relation, there exist numbers $a > 0$, $b > 0$ such that $aC_1 \, \tau_k \, bC_2$ (a and b being the prices of C_1 and C_2 in the money-commodity). By 'equating' the different products of their labour 'to each other in exchange as values'—or more accurately, in placing them in a money relation τ_k—people 'equate their different kinds of labour as human labour'—or more accurately, they place the differing complexes of labour in a relation Θ defined solely within the space of the concrete labours. In short,

Now, if the relation Θ of 'equating' is similar to the customary equation in that like quantities may be subtracted from both sides without destroying the relation, then we may conclude:

From $(5a\,M\text{-labour}, 3a\,S\text{-labour}) \, \Theta \, (2.5b\,M\text{-labour}, 7.5b\,S\text{-labour})$

it follows that

$$(5a-2.5b) \ M\text{-labour} \ \Theta \ (7.5b-3a) \ S\text{-labour}$$

and if the relation Θ is homogeneous like an ordinary equation, then

$$1 \ M\text{-labour} \ \Theta \ \alpha \ S\text{-labour}$$

where $\alpha = \dfrac{7.5b-3a}{5a-2.5b}$ or $\alpha = \dfrac{7.5z-3}{5-3.5z}$

where $z = \dfrac{b}{a}$ is the exchange ratio, or more precisely, the relative price of coal and iron. (The conclusions drawn here will be examined in greater detail when we consider the more general case.)

Thus, not only the aggregate complexes of labour but also the individual concrete labours themselves are 'equated'. The measure α in which this occurs is linked in a determinate way to z, the relative price of the two commodities. Solving this equation for z, we have

$$z = \frac{5\alpha + 3}{2.5\alpha + 7.5} \ .$$

Graphically, this relation is depicted in fig. 23. The relative

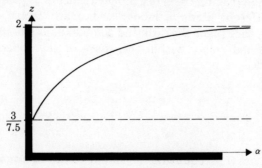

Figure 23

price, z, of coal to iron thus rises with a rising weight of mining to smelting (α). But because of the interconnection of production, this relation is not linear. Since α can assume meaningful values only between 0 and $+ \infty$, it follows that the relative price

z must always lie between $\dfrac{3}{7.5}$ and 2. If z were 4, for example, the complex x would be equated with the complex $4y$, and since $4y \geq 2x$, it would be equated with more than double itself, which is obviously not a realistic relation between expenditures of labour. In any event, the relation between z and α is only restricted to a certain range; it is *not* pegged to a *specific* quantity.

Concrete labour 'equated' through the relation Θ is called abstract labour. By virtue of the relation Θ—or as we may now say, abstract labour—the concrete labours differ only quantitatively, in accordance with the coefficients α. From the 'equating'

$$1 \ M\text{-labour} \ \Theta \ \alpha \ S\text{-labour}$$

it follows that the complexes x and y are also 'equated' with a certain quantity of S-labour, namely

$$x \ \Theta \ (5\alpha + 3) \ S\text{-labour and } y \ \Theta \ (2.5\alpha + 7.5) \ S\text{-labour.}$$

If we now denote the quantities of S-labour to which the complexes x and y respectively correspond under the relation Θ as

$$\lambda_1 = 5\alpha + 3$$

$$\lambda_2 = 2.5\alpha + 7.5$$

then the relation between z and α can be reformulated as

$$z = \frac{\lambda_1}{\lambda_2} \ .$$

λ_1 and λ_2 indicate the social expenditures of labour for coal and iron respectively as abstract labour, here expressed in terms of smelting-labour. Later we will examine these quantities, which we shall call labour-values, more closely. For the moment, several of their characteristics can already be listed.

First, abstract-labour has no time dimension: it must always be expressed as a quantity of some concrete, albeit arbitrary, labour. 'One hour of abstract labour' therefore has no meaning, while 'one hour of carpentry' does.

Second, the quantities λ_1 and λ_2 of abstract labour are still doubly indeterminate: they depend both on which concrete labour serves as the measure and on how large α is.

Third, the ratio $\dfrac{\lambda_1}{\lambda_2}$ does not itself depend on which concrete labour is taken as the measure of abstract labour (it should be evident that while λ_1 and λ_2 would change if smelting were chosen as the measure instead of mining, the ratio would not). But $\dfrac{\lambda_1}{\lambda_2}$ does, on the other hand, depend on α.

A moment's reflection about these complications reveals that the expression $z = \dfrac{\lambda_1}{\lambda_2}$ means quite simply: relative price and relative labour-value coincide.

2. General Derivation of the Analytic Concept of Abstract Labour

Let us begin as we did in chapter 4, with the production of n commodities through n different concrete labours. Let τ be a homogeneous one-one relation, as described in chapter 3, section 1. A *complex* of concrete labours $x = (x_1 \text{ type } 1, x_2 \text{ type } 2, \ldots, x_n \text{ type } n)$ is an element of the space (more accurately: the cone) of concrete labours $\mathfrak{R}^n_+$ spanned by the individual concrete labours. Such a complex will henceforth be denoted by $x = (x_1, x_2, \ldots, x_n)$ for short. Now let a relation Θ be defined on this space, as follows.

For $x, y \; \varepsilon \; \mathfrak{R}^n_+$, $x \; \Theta \; y$ if and only if the following two conditions hold.

(1) There are quantities of commodities aC_i, bC_j from C such that

$$x \to aC_i$$
$$y \to bC_j \quad \text{(in the sense of chapter 4)}$$

(2) There is a quantity of commodity cC_k from C such that

$$aC_i \; \tau \; cC_k \text{ and } bC_j \; \tau \; cC_k$$

(or $aC_i \; \tau_k \; bC_j$ as in chapter 3, section 1).

These conditions may be interpreted thus: Two complexes of concrete labours stand in the relation Θ if they are

(1) the social expenditures of labour for two quantities of commodities, which are

(2) 'equated' with the same quantity of a third commodity (with respect to τ)

If C_k is a money-commodity, then we may simply say: Two complexes of concrete labours stand in the relation Θ if each is objectified in the same quantity of money (of a money-commodity).

To make sure that the second condition is met, we must assume that at least one money-commodity exists. If τ is a symmetric value relation, all commodities are money-commodities (chapter 3, section 1, Proposition 3). τ is a transitive value-relation if and only if all commodities are money-commodities, and moreover all money-commodities occupy this same money-relation (chapter 3, section 1, Proposition 4). Since one aim of our approach to abstract labour is to resolve the problem of transitivity, we will begin with an exchange-structure that is not necessarily consistent; in other words, τ is not necessarily transitive. Money-commodities with different money relations may therefore exist. Although any money-commodity defines a consistent exchange-structure (since τ_k is transitive), two different money-commodities may give rise to conflicting exchange-structures. (See chapter 3, section 1 on the duality of money-commodities in the two-country example. 'Theoretically', in the most extreme case each commodity-owner would consider his own commodity a money-commodity and trade in accordance with his 'own' corresponding system of relative prices.) Since *all* money-commodities play a role in the definition of Θ unless a particular money-commodity is specified, it cannot be assumed in advance that Θ is transitive, since the conflict between money-commodities could penetrate production. Nevertheless, Θ does possess the following *properties*.

(a) Θ is symmetric.

(b) Θ is homogeneous.

(c)   Let $v_i = (v_{1i}l_1,\ v_{2i}l_2, \ldots,\ v_{ni}l_n)$, the social expenditure of concrete labours to produce one unit of C_i for $i = 1, \ldots, n$. The v_i are linearly independent, and for $i, j = 1, \ldots, n$

$$v_i \,\Theta\, v_i \text{ and}$$

for i and j there exists an
$a > 0$ such that $v_i \,\Theta\, av_j$.

Demonstration.   (a) follows immediately from the definition of Θ.

(b)   follows from the assumption of constant returns to scale and the homogeneity of τ.

(c)   can be obtained as follows: v_i is the i-th column of the matrix LV. Since L is a diagonal matrix with positive entries in the diagonal, it is invertible. Since V is invertible by definition (see chapter 4), so is LV, and the v_i are therefore linearly independent. Since from chapter 4 we know that $v_i \rightarrow 1C_i$ and at least one money-commodity exists, it follows from the definition of Θ that $v_i \,\Theta\, v_i$. Since $v_i \rightarrow 1C_i$ and $v_j \rightarrow 1C_j$, and because of the existence of a money-commodity C_k, there exist $\bar{a}, \bar{b} > 0$ such that $\bar{a}C_i \,\tau_k\, \bar{b}C_j$; then $\bar{a}v_i \rightarrow \bar{a}C_i$, $\bar{b}v_j \rightarrow \bar{b}C_j$, and therefore $\bar{a}v_i \,\Theta\, \bar{b}v_j$; thus, since Θ is homogeneous, $v_i \,\Theta\, av_j$, where $a = \dfrac{\bar{b}}{\bar{a}} > 0$.

These simple properties of Θ result essentially from the fact that this relation between complexes of labour is induced by a relation between quantities of commodities. If Θ is meaningfully to depict a social 'equating' of expenditures of labour, this relation must have other properties as well. (For example, it does not follow from anything said so far that Θ is reflexive.) Let us therefore make the following assumptions, which have to do solely with the character of Θ as an 'equating' of complexes of labour and not with the relation on quantities of commodities.

Θ *is non-trivial*: for $x \, \varepsilon \, \Re^{n}_{+}$, $0 \, \Theta \, x$ only if $x = 0$

Θ *is monotonic*: let $x, y, u, v \, \varepsilon \, \Re^{n}_{+}$, and $x \, \Theta \, y$. Then $u \, \Theta \, v$ if and only if $(x + u) \, \Theta \, (y + v)$.

Interpretation. Non-triviality states that labour (of whatever kind) cannot be 'equated' with non-labour. If this condition were not met, then because of the homogeneity of Θ, some suitable multiples of a complex of labour would not count socially as labour, and this makes no sense, since all the concrete labours being considered here are socially necessary for the production of one of the commodities. Monotonicity means that if two complexes count as 'equal', then so do the complexes obtained by the addition or subtraction of two 'equal-counting' complexes from them. Monotonicity, unlike non-triviality, is an essential assumption. An 'equating' without this property would make little sense. If Θ is monotonic, then non-triviality is equivalent to this: if $x \, \Theta \, x$, $x \, \Theta \, y$, and $x \leq y$, then $x = y$. In other words: two complexes one of which uses at least as much of every type of labour as the other and more of one type of labour do not count as 'equal'. 'Equating' in the customary sense of the equals sign is both non-trivial and monotonic, although these properties are then so obvious that they go unnoticed. (On both assumptions, consider the operations carried out under Θ in the coal-iron example.)

Properties (a)-(c) of Θ, combined with non-triviality and monotonicity, yield a number of propositions.

Proposition 1. Θ is an equivalence relation on $\Re^{n}_{+}$, and there exist uniquely determined coefficients $\alpha_{ij} > 0$ for $i, j = 1, 2, \ldots n$, such that

1 hour of labour of type $i \, \Theta \, \alpha_{ij}$ hours of labour of type j

Demonstration. The properties of Θ and the two assumptions fulfil the requirements for Proposition 6 in part 2 of the mathematical appendix. It follows from this proposition that Θ is an equivalence relation, and since the components of the identity vector (e_i) immediately correspond to the individual concrete labours, the existence of unique coefficients $\alpha_{ij} > 0$ follows.

The equivalence relation Θ is called the *relation of abstract labour*, and the coefficients α_{ij}, which indicate the relative weight of one concrete labour to another in accordance with this relation, will be called the *reduction-coefficients*.

Proposition 6 of the mathematical appendix further yields:

Proposition 2: If for $x \; \varepsilon \; \Re^n_+ \;\; f_j(x) = \sum\limits_{h=1}^{n} x_h \, \alpha_{hj}$ for $j = 1, \ldots, n$, then

$x \Theta y$ if and only if $f_j(x) = f_j(y)$ for some $j = 1, \ldots, n$.

For a complex x of concrete labours, $f_j(x)$ represents the appropriate *quantity of abstract labour* expressed in terms of concrete labour of type j. Proposition 2 states that the equivalence classes under the relation of abstract labour correspond to precisely one quantity of abstract labour each (regardless of the type of concrete labour in which this is expressed). The complexes $x = v_i$ are of particular interest. The quantity of abstract labour

$$\lambda_{ij} = f_j(v_i) = \sum\limits_{h=1}^{n} v_{hi} l_h \alpha_{hj}$$

is called the labour-value (or for short, the *value*) of a unit of commodity C_i, expressed in labour of type j.

For a money-commodity C_k, let z_{ik} be the price of C_i in terms of this money-commodity. Then we have:

Proposition 3: For any two commodities C_i, C_j, any money-commodity C_k, and any type of labour g,

$$\frac{z_{ik}}{z_{jk}} = \frac{\lambda_{ig}}{\lambda_{jg}}.$$

Demonstration. If $z(v_i, v_j)$ is the uniquely determined coefficient such that $v_i \Theta z(v_i, v_j) v_j$, then (by Proposition 6 of part 2 of the mathematical appendix)

$$z(v_i, v_j) = \frac{f_g(v_i)}{f_g(v_j)} = \frac{\lambda_{ig}}{\lambda_{jg}}.$$

As in the proof of property (c) of Θ, for a money-commodity C_k: since $C_i \tau z_{ik} C_k$ and $C_j \tau z_{jk} C_k$, and because $v_i \rightarrow C_i$, $v_j \rightarrow C_j$ by the definition of Θ and the homogeneity of τ, $z_{jk} v_i \Theta z_{ik} v_j$; hence because $z(v_i, v_j)$ is uniquely determined,

$$z(v_i, v_j) = \frac{z_{ik}}{z_{jk}} \ .$$

Consequently, together

$$\frac{z_{ik}}{z_{jk}} = \frac{\lambda_{ig}}{\lambda_{jg}} \ .$$

This proposition yields the following answer to the problem of *transitivity*. All money-commodities induce the same system of relative prices, and hence the same money relation. Since Θ does not depend on a specific money-commodity—*all* money-commodities enter into Θ—and, since from Proposition 1 the reduction-coefficients are uniquely determined by Θ, it follows from Proposition 2 that the λ_{ig} do not depend on k; Proposition 3 tells us that $\frac{z_{ik}}{z_{jk}}$ does not depend on k either, and this is true for all money-commodities. In particular, if all commodities are money-commodities, it follows from Proposition 3 that τ itself is a transitive value relation (from Proposition 4, chapter 3, section 1). This situation can be interpreted as follows. Considered in their own framework alone, that of quantities of commodities, different money-commodities will inevitably induce different money relations. But these relations are, so to speak, suspended in a vacuum so long as they are not linked to the production of commodities by means of labour. Now, in the context of concrete labours, every money relation induces its own 'equating' of complexes of labour, which because of the interconnecton of production and the division of labour encompasses all concrete labours. In short, any money relation induces a generalized social relation on the space of concrete labours. Two complexes of labour, representing social expenditures, however, will be socially 'equated' in only one way, described in the non-triviality and monotonicity of Θ. The monotonicity of Θ is an essential reason why Θ is an equivalence

90

relation, and hence grounds Proposition 3. Conversely, if Proposition 3 did not hold, then the 'equating' would not be monotonic (or Θ would be trivial; all its other properties would remain intact). In that case it would be better not to speak of 'abstract labour' (as in the two-country example in chapter 3, section 1).

A further, in a sense twofold, conclusion from Proposition 3 is that since $\dfrac{z_{ik}}{z_{jk}}$ does not depend on g, neither does $\dfrac{\lambda_{ig}}{\lambda_{jg}}$. The *relative* labour-values of commodities are thus independent of the concrete labour in which abstract labour is expressed. But relative labour-value, and hence relative price, does essentially depend on the reduction-coefficients. This dependency, which entails certain constraints on relative prices, will be examined more closely below.

3. The Exchange Curve

In what follows the subscripts k and g for the money-commodity C_k and a type of labour g respectively will be dropped for the sake of brevity. Price, previously z_{ik}, will be denoted by p_i; α_i takes the place of α_{ig} and λ_i replaces λ_{ig}.

Proposition 3 can then be written:

For any two commodities C_i and C_j, $\dfrac{p_i}{p_j} = \dfrac{\lambda_i}{\lambda_j}$

This relation is fundamental for the connection of circulation (relative price) and production (relative labour-value); let us then so name it: the *fundamental relation*. It is not an *ad hoc* assumption about the connection between circulation and production, but a necessary consequence of the concept of abstract labour developed here.[2] Since labour-values depend (apart from the production-structure) only on the vector $\alpha = (\alpha_1, \ldots, \alpha_n)$ of the reduction-coefficients, the fundamental relation yields the following representation of the exchange ratio $\dfrac{p_i}{p_j}$ as dependent on α:

$$\frac{p_i}{p_j}(\alpha) = \frac{\sum\limits_{h=1}^{n} v_{hi} l_h \alpha_h}{\sum\limits_{h=1}^{n} v_{hj} l_h \alpha_h}$$

This relation, which describes the movement of exchange ratios depending on the relative weights of the concrete labours as shares of abstract labour within a fixed production-structure, may be called the *exchange curve* (cf. the particular curve for the coal-iron example above).

Proposition 6 from part 2 of the mathematical appendix yields the following approximation of the exchange curve.

Proposition 4.   For any two commodities C_i, C_j, and any $\alpha \, \varepsilon \, \mathfrak{R}_+^n$

$$\min_{1 \le h \le n} \frac{v_{hi}}{v_{hj}} \le \frac{p_i}{p_j}(\alpha) \le \max_{1 \le h \le n} \frac{v_{hi}}{v_{hj}}$$

By using the magnitude $\sigma(A)$ introduced in part 1 of the mathematical appendix for a production-structure, the limits common to *all* pairs of commodities can be indicated.

Proposition 5.   For any two commodities C_i, C_j and any $\alpha \, \varepsilon \, \mathfrak{R}_+^n$

$$\sigma(A') \le \frac{p_i}{p_j}(\alpha) \le \frac{1}{\sigma(A')}$$

Demonstration.   Applying the definition of σ to the transpose matrix A', we have (see lemma in the mathematical appendix)

$$\sigma(A') = \min_{1 \le i, j, h \le n} \frac{v_{hi}}{v_{hj}}.$$

Hence, $\sigma(A') \le \min\limits_{1 \le h \le n} \frac{v_{hi}}{v_{hj}}$ for all indices i, j, whence Proposition 5 is obtained from Proposition 4.

If $\sigma(A) = 0$ for the production-structure, then also $\sigma(A') = 0$, and Proposition 5 yields only trivial limits. (See mathematical appendix, part 1, on the relation between $\sigma(A)$ and $\sigma(A')$ and the following arguments.) But if $\sigma(A) > 0$, and hence also $\sigma(A') > 0$, then Proposition 5 will yield genuine limits for the movement of all exchange ratios. $\sigma(A) > 0$ if and only if the production-structure is connected. Thus: in a connected production-structure, the exchange ratios $\frac{p_i}{p_j}$ can fluctuate only within certain limits set by the production-structure. But Proposition 5 does not establish any particular exchange ratio; it simply determines a limited latitude for a given curve. The larger $\sigma(A')$ (and $0 \leq \sigma(A') \leq 1$ always), the narrower this latitude is. The limiting case, in which the exchange curve imposes exactly one exchange ratio, occurs if and only if $\sigma(A') = \frac{1}{\sigma(A')}$, hence when $\sigma(A') = 1$. This occurs if and only if $n = 1$, in other words, if only one commodity is produced by means of this same commodity and a particular type of labour: that is, if there is no social division of labour. In general, it is to be expected that there will be a social division of labour and a strong link among the separate labours, and in that case $0 < \sigma(A) < 1$. Then the exchange ratios are not determined by the production-structure, but can vary only within certain limits. The greater the links of the socially divided labours, the narrower is the scope for latitude.

The concept of the exchange curve can be illustrated by a number of simple examples.

1. *Coal-iron.* The exchange curve here has already been given. Its limits in general can be represented as follows.

Since $V = \begin{pmatrix} \dfrac{5}{2} & \dfrac{5}{4} \\ & \\ 1 & \dfrac{5}{2} \end{pmatrix}$, $\displaystyle\min_{h=1,2} \frac{v_{h1}}{v_{h2}} = \min(2, \tfrac{2}{5}) = \tfrac{2}{5} = \tfrac{3}{7.5}$

and $\displaystyle\max_{h=1,2} \frac{v_{h1}}{v_{h2}} = \max(2, \tfrac{2}{5}) = 2$. $\sigma(A')$ is therefore $\tfrac{2}{5}$, and the universal limits are $\tfrac{2}{5}$ and $\tfrac{5}{2}$.

2. *Sraffa's beans example.*[3] This is of the form

$$A = \begin{pmatrix} a & b \\ 0 & c \end{pmatrix} \quad \text{where } 0 \leq a < c < 1,$$

$$L = \begin{pmatrix} l_1 & 0 \\ 0 & l_2 \end{pmatrix}$$

The exchange curve has the form

$$\frac{p_1}{p_2}(\alpha) = \frac{(1-c)\, l_1 \cdot \dfrac{\alpha_1}{\alpha_2}}{b\, l_1 \cdot \dfrac{\alpha_1}{\alpha_2} + (1-a)\, l_2}$$

The exchange curve is depicted in fig. 24. $\sigma(A') = \sigma(A) = 0$, and the universal limits are therefore trivial.

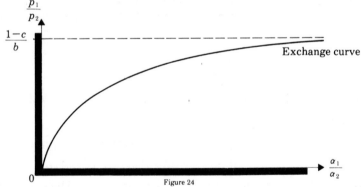

Figure 24

3. *Smith's deer-beaver example.*[4] Here we have

$$A = \begin{pmatrix} 0 & 0 \\ 0 & 0 \end{pmatrix}, L = \begin{pmatrix} l_1 & 0 \\ 0 & l_2 \end{pmatrix}.$$

The exchange curve has the form

$$\frac{p_1}{p_2}(\alpha) = \frac{l_1}{l_2} \cdot \frac{\alpha_1}{\alpha_2}.$$

The exchange curve is shown in fig. 25. $\sigma(A') = \sigma(A) = 0$, and the universal limits are therefore trivial.

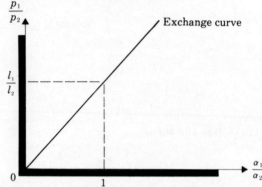

Figure 25

The essential difference between the first example and the two others is that the production-structure is connected in the first, but not in the others. Proposition 5 tells us that in a connected production-structure the exchange curve for any pair of commodities C_i, C_j cannot be a straight line (dependent on one reduction-coefficient). This is characteristic for such a structure.

In the second example the exchange curve for $\frac{p_1}{p_2}$ is not a straight line, but it would be for $\frac{p_2}{p_1}$. In the third, it is a straight line for both $\frac{p_1}{p_2}$ and $\frac{p_2}{p_1}$. The difference between the second and and third examples is that in the second there is an upper limit (for $\frac{p_1}{p_2}$) and a lower limit (for $\frac{p_2}{p_1}$), whereas in the third, since the production-structure is not connected at all, the exchange ratio has no limits. Sraffa's and Smith's examples are instructive in various respects, and we will return to them later. The deer-beaver example in particular will feature in the critique of the classical labour theory of value.

The conclusions reached in this chapter can be summarized as follows.

1. The money relation (more generally, the value-form) for products of labour results in the 'equating' of certain quantities

of the various concrete labours expended in production. This 'equating' is precisely described by an equivalence relation Θ on the space of the concrete labours induced through the money relation and by the reduction-coefficients a_{ij}. Concrete labour in the equivalence relation Θ is called abstract labour.

2. Every quantity of produced commodities represents a quantity of abstract labour, a labour-value (in abstract labour). But this is only a qualitative, not quantitative, determination, since labour-value remains doubly undetermined. It depends on the concrete labour in which this quantity of abstract labour is expressed, and even more important, on the reduction-coefficients. Simultaneous with the derivation of the concept of abstract labour, the equality of relative price and relative labour-value—also a purely qualitative relation—emerged as a fundamental relation between circulation and production.

3. Two consequences for circulation follow from the fundamental relation: an answer to the transitivity problem and, in the form of the exchange curve, a limitation on the magnitudes of circulation. Relative prices can move only within certain limits, which depend on the interconnections of the production-structure.

The role of abstract labour in terms of the basic question raised at the beginning of this chapter can now be formulated more simply. The concrete labour expended in production has the form of abstract labour (in a market economy), because the regulation of social labour occurs through the circulation of the products of labour by means of money; and circulation acquires its consistency because it is labour in the form of abstract labour that is being 'circulated' with the commodities.

So far the quantitative side of abstract labour has remained unexplored. Consideration of it will begin in the next chapter.

6
The Value-Structure
of Production

It was shown in the previous chapter that individual units of commodities could be assigned quantities of abstract labour λ_{ij}, so-called labour-values, thus:

$$\lambda_{ij} = \sum_{h=1}^{n} v_{hi} l_h \alpha_{hj}.$$

If the concrete labour of type j is held fixed, we can dispense with the index j, as we did in the last chapter, and the equation can be rewritten

$$\lambda_i = \sum_{h=1}^{n} v_{hi} l_h \alpha_h.$$

where λ_i is the labour-value of a unit of C_i and α_h the reduction-coefficient of labour of type h (expressed in type j). Since v_{ii}, l_i, and α_i are all positive, $\lambda_i > 0$ for every $i = 1, \ldots n$. The above system of equations will be denoted the *value-system*. If λ is the vector of the λ_i, α the vector of the α_h and $L = \mathrm{diag}\, l$, the value-system can be written in matrix form as

$$\lambda = \alpha L V \quad \text{or} \quad \lambda = \alpha L (I - A)^{-1}$$

since $\qquad V = (I - A)^{-1}$ (see chapter 4).

This value-system, based on the concept of abstract labour, now makes it possible to describe production itself in these terms. The basic question of this chapter then becomes: How can the production of commodities, hitherto formulated in terms of physical quantities, be described as value-production in the light of the character of labour as abstract labour? What are the relevant value magnitudes in such a description?

Clearly, not only the commodity inputs, which are already included in the value-system, but also the labour inputs of various types must be encompassed as values. Before this is done, in the form of labour-power as a particular commodity, the value-system as formulated above should be critically distinguished from classical labour theory of value and its contemporary variants.

1. Critique of Classical/Contemporary Labour Theory of Value

The core of this 'doctrine of the utmost importance for political economy' (Ricardo) has already been revealed in the simple example from the 'early and rude state of society' (Smith): the deer-beaver economy.[1] This example considers a society of hunters in which the killing of a beaver as a rule 'costs' twice the labour needed to kill a deer; one beaver therefore exchanges for two deer, which means that one beaver is worth twice as much as one deer. To analyse this example, let us express it in the terms we have been using.

(a)   It is assumed that deer and beaver are *exchanged*; there is thus a relation

$$1 \text{ beaver } \tau\ z \text{ deer, such that } z > 0.$$

(Money relations and similar considerations are not required in this simple example; τ represents direct exchange.)

(b)   The production-relations are

$$l_1 \text{ hours of beaver-hunting} \rightarrow 1 \text{ beaver}$$

$$l_2 \text{ hours of deer-hunting} \rightarrow 1 \text{ deer}$$

with $l_1 = 2 \cdot l_2$.
(Since no means of production are used, $A = 0$.)

(c) From (a) and (b) we obtain an 'equating' of the concrete labours 'beaver-hunting' and 'deer-hunting', namely

l_1 hours beaver-hunting $\ominus$ $z \cdot l_2$ hours deer-hunting;

hence

1 hour beaver-hunting $\ominus$ α hours deer-hunting

with the reduction-coefficient

$$\alpha = \frac{zl_2}{l_1} = \frac{1}{2}z.$$

The exchange-curve is therefore $z = 2\alpha$ (cf. chapter 5, section 3), graphically represented in fig. 26.

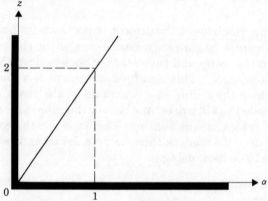

Figure 26

Now, the intention of classical labour theory of value is clearly to show not only that an exchange *curve* is possible, but also that an exchange *point* will be realized: $z = 2$ and $\alpha = 1$. But why this specific exchange ratio and no other of the endless abundance of possible ratios? What particular feature of the society in question leads straight to this ratio? Before considering the reasons why—which relate to the assumption of homogeneous labour and a faulty analysis of the value-form—let us examine a version of the classical idea still prevalent today.[2]

The difference between the classical and current version is really only that the latter deals with more than two products and takes means of production into account, although only as circulating capital, since the introduction of fixed capital entails serious difficulties.[3] It is assumed that each unit of a commodity embodies a certain quantity of labour μ_i, composed of the addition of directly expended labour and the quantities contained in the means of production. Thus

$$\mu_i = \sum_{h=1}^{n} a_{hi}\mu_h + l_i$$

in matrix notation: $\quad \mu = l(I-A)^{-1}$.

(Where A is productive, and μ is the vector of the μ_i.) These classical labour values μ_i are thus determined by the technical structure of production alone, by A and l, independent of the mode of distribution, specific to a market society. A comparison with labour-values based on abstract labour as formulated above shows that $\lambda_i = \mu_i$ if and only if $\alpha_i = 1$, for every i (with some fixed concrete labour as the measure of abstract labour). Both these remarks thus correspond to what was already established in the deer-beaver example.

Now, turning to the critique of the classical/contemporary labour theory of value, let us examine two themes: the specific coordination of concrete labours and the dogma of homogeneous labour.

Specific coordination of concrete labour

Let us consider a society in which the manufacture of products is based on a division of labour, and in which the products of labour are not merely consumed, but also serve as means of production such that the production-structure is productive (cf. the general model in chapter 1).

In accordance with chapter 4, the expenditures of labour of different types in society as a whole (per unit of production) is represented by

$$(v_{1i} l_1, v_{2i} l_2, \ldots, v_{ni} l_n) \to C_i.$$

This indicates first that labour is required and more precisely, which concrete labours are technically required for the production of a given additional unit of product—in the case of C_i *all* those of types of labour h such that $v_{hi} > 0$, not only labour of type i. On the basis of these social labours, separate but nevertheless interconnected in this manner, some coordination of the individual concrete labours is required. Thus, if an additional amount x_i of C_i is to be manufactured, what is needed is not only the quantity $x_h l_h$ of labour of type h directly required for the production of $x_h C_h$, but rather a quantity of labour of type h given by the expression $\sum_{i=1}^{n} x_i v_{hi} l_h$. Because of the division of labour, however, there is no reason to suppose that the labour of type h expended only for the production of the *specific* product C_h will actually occur in the amount needed to meet the social demand expressed in $x_1, x_2, \ldots, x_n$; this requires some coordination of the individual concrete labours, however effected. Nearly all societies have in common that labour is necessary and that a coordination is required. But *how* is labour to be done and such a coordination effected? Therein lie the essential differences among various societies. The most varied mechanisms of coordination have arisen throughout history, either evolving further or withering away. In some, labour was coordinated rather indirectly, through god and his laws (some labours pleasing god, others the devil); others effected the task more directly, through kinship or despotism (see the discussion in chapter 1).[4] The characteristic form of coordination for a market society, analysed in chapters 2 and 3, is the value-form and the money relation between products of labour, from which it emerged (chapter 5) that in a market economy the individual concrete labours are socially coordinated as abstract labour. The deer-beaver example speaks of a hunting people, but there is no mention of the form in which concrete labours are coordinated (even assuming that exchange be a method of coordination), so that the reduction-coefficient automatically remains 'naturally' undetermined. If anything, exchange is not a relevant form of coordination for a 'hunting people', religious ritual or clan structures generally playing this role, but in economic theory, hunting peoples exist so as to animate market economies.

The contemporary formulation of classical labour theory of

value has forsaken hunting peoples. But although market economies are considered, the corresponding mechanisms of coordination are not examined, and labour-values appear as raw technical magnitudes, with no analysis of the value-form. In short, as Marx himself was aware, in both cases the approach is ahistorical, not specific to the form of society in question.

The dogma of homogeneous labour

In the light of abstract labour, we can see that both the classical and contemporary labour theory of value assume that all the reduction-coefficients are equal—indeed equal to 1. In other words, it is assumed that concrete labour is homogeneous. Some formulations even consider only one type of labour, which is clearly absurd given a division of labour. It is conceivable that certain assumptions about the mechanism of coordination could *produce* equal reduction-coefficients. But the classical/ contemporary labour theory of value does not formulate such assumptions, so the homogeneity is a mere dogma. This dogma has a venerable history and is found in the most diverse approaches, with the most varied consequences.[5] Unlike the concept of abstract labour, the supposition of homogeneous labour supplants any analysis of the specific coordination of concrete labours—in this case, analysis of the value-form and money—with a theoretical fiction about the character of human labour. The consequence for the classical/contemporary labour theory of value is that technical labour-values are detached from socially specific coordination magnitudes like prices; the bond between values and prices is thereby severed, and the now immortal transformation problem is born.

2. The Special Commodity Labour-Power

The production of commodities in a market economy can proceed in the manner of the model discussed in chapter 1 only if not only the means of production, but also the labour-power required to effect the concrete labours can be purchased on the market. The purchase and sale of labour-power in a market economy occur principally through a money-commodity (although exceptions are possible). Justification of this assertion could be based in part on the analytic investigations of chapter 3, but it must also take due note of the historical persistence of the commodity-nature of labour-power. For the moment, however, we will forgo a detailed study of the purchase and sale of labour-power.[6]

The important thing is that labour-power is a special commodity, radically different in two respects from the commodities we have considered so far. First, the commodity (labour-power) and commodity owner (the worker) are united in one individual; a worker can neither own nor sell the labour-power of another, nor can a number of workers collectively own and sell labour-power (although it is collectively set to work in production). Second, unlike other commodities, labour-power is not manufactured industrially—at least, not yet. The production of this commodity consists in its reproduction. The *reproduction* of labour-power is a difficult matter, not least because a legal individual, and in the end a flesh-and-blood human being, is perforce reproduced along with the commodity. Here again we will limit ourselves to one specific aspect, symbolized in fig. 27.

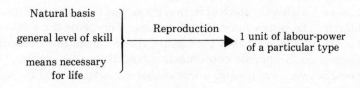

Figure 27

Even this simple diagram includes 'aspects'—such as a natural basis (factors like health or even climate) and general level of skill (like education, but also language)—that are not easily amenable to more precise analysis. Let us therefore focus only on the reproduction of labour-power through the means required to sustain life, which can be represented as the produced commodities $C_1, \ldots, C_n$. This will suffice for our purposes. The reproduction of labour-power implies a second feedback mechanism for the model in chapter 1. (See fig. 28.)

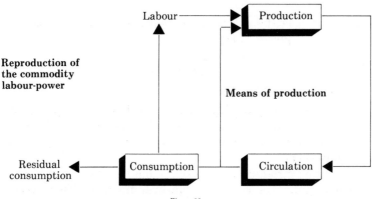

Figure 28

What is essential is that a portion of the commodities produced, of whatever type and quantity, must be consigned to the reproduction of labour-power. The category 'residual consumption' comprises that part of consumption not devoted to the reproduction of labour-power (like consumption by non-workers, 'luxuries', and so on). The distinction is quite relative, serving only to depict the division of consumption into two components. Let it simply be noted that the double feedback to the two 'switching points' of investment and consumption is of prominent importance for the dynamic of a market economy (as the accelerator and multiplier). The reproduction of n types of labour-power can be represented as follows.

Relations of reproduction

$(b_{1i} C_1, \ldots, b_{ni} C_n) \to 1$ hour of labour-power of type i for every $i = 1, \ldots, n$, where b_{ji} is the number of units of the commodity C_j that enter into the reproduction of one hour of labour-power of type i, and thus $b_{ji} \geq 0$. Let the b_{ji} be arranged in an $n \times n$ matrix B. (Where this can be done without misunderstanding, the additional $C_1, \ldots, C_n$ will be omitted from the left side of the reproduction relations, and the right side will be shortened to type i.)

By means of the reproduction relations the commodity labour-power can be assigned a *re*production-value and a *re*production-price as follows:

$$\sum_{j=1}^{n} b_{ji}\lambda_j \quad \text{is the } \textit{reproduction-value} \text{ of one hour of labour-power of type } i$$

$$\sum_{j=1}^{n} b_{ji}p_j \quad \text{is the } \textit{reproduction-price} \text{ of one hour of labour-power of type } i$$

Since there are quite different conceptions of the *particularity* of the commodity labour-power, a few remarks may forestall any misunderstanding of the relations of *re*production as formulated here.

First, the reproduction relations should *not* be understood as a means of subsistence theory, however modified. The matrix B is intended only to depict the simple fact that labour-power must be reproduced. *No assumptions* are made about the structure of B or the magnitude of its elements; in other words, no assumptions about *which* commodities are really necessary (for which j is $b_{ji} > 0$) or about *what amounts* of these commodities are required for various labour-powers (the magnitudes of the b_{ji}). In short, matrix B is a *variable*.

Second, it would not correspond to the character of a market economy to proceed on the basis of a 'structure of real wages', with or without historical caveats, since the price of labour-power is paid as money-wages. Price and reproduction-price are two different things: if w_i denotes the hourly wage-rate for labour-power of type i, and $w_i^r = \sum_{j=1}^{n} b_{ji}p_j$ its reproduction-price, then it may be that $w_i = w_i^r$, but $w_i < w_i^r$ and $w_i > w_i^r$ are also possible. If we first disregard as an exceptional occurrence the case in which $w_i < w_i^r$ (an assumption requiring justification) and denote the saved (or simply not-spent) portion of the wage as w_i^s, then we may write

$$w_i = w_i^s + w_i^r.$$

But this should not be taken to mean that the wage is determined by the b_{ji}. A (strict) subsistence theory of wages would assume that $w_i^s = 0$ and that w_i^r is determined by the b_{ji}. Here, in contrast to such a procedure, B is a *dependent* variable.[7]

Third, the fundamental relation does trivially induce the equality of relative *re*production-value and relative *re*production-price. But in the light of the second remark above, the relative price of the commodity labour-power, $\dfrac{w_i}{w_j}$, and its relative reproduction-value are not assumed to be equal. In accordance with its derivation, the fundamental relation holds only for (industrially) *produced* commodities, but not for the special commodity labour-power (and its relative price). Moreover, an extension of the concept of 'value' as derived in chapter 5 to labour-power is not possible. In short: the *re*production relations for the commodity labour-power do not allow it to be treated like a produced commodity.

3. Surplus-Value and the Reproduction Curve

The value-system $\lambda = \alpha L (I-A)^{-1}$ permits vectors of quantities of commodities to be considered as values, and thus as quantities of abstract labour. Since the magnitude of the reduction-coefficients is not yet determined (it will be in chapter 7), these quantities are treated as dependent on α. Aggregate social values will subsequently be considered, i.e. we establish a suitable but fixed vector x of activities $x_i \geq 0$ $(i = 1, \ldots, n)$ for all sectors of production. To avoid tedious summations, these will be presented in compact matrix form.

The total expenditure of means of production will be given by the vector Ax. Since x also indicates the gross output of the individual commodities, the *net* social product is

$$y = x - Ax = (I-A)x.$$

(That is, $y_i = x_i - \sum\limits_{j=1}^{n} a_{ij}x_j$ is the net product of C_i for $i = 1$, $2, \ldots, n$. Since we are now dealing only with aggregate social magnitudes, the qualification 'aggregate social' will be omitted.)

If A is productive, which we will assume, there will be at least one positive net product; in other words, there exists an $x \geq 0$ such that for the corresponding net product y, $y > 0$. (In general, not every net product is positive; cf. mathematical appendix, part 1.)

The total expenditure of means of reproduction is given by BLx. Subtraction of this expenditure from the net product yields the *surplus product*

$$u = x - Ax - BLx = (I - A - BL)x$$

(The net and surplus products are therefore vectors.)

The system as a whole will be called capable of self-reproduction, or *self-reproductive* for short, if there exists a vector $x \geq 0$ of activities such that the corresponding surplus product $u \geq 0$; it is called strictly self-reproductive if $u > 0$.

On the basis of the expression

$$(v_{1i} l_1 \text{ type } 1, \ldots, v_{ni} l_n \text{ type } n) \rightarrow C_i \text{ for } i = 1, \ldots n$$

(see chapter 4), the surplus product represents socially surplus labour; indeed, u directly represents surplus labour of type h in the amount $\sum_{i=1}^{n} v_{hi} l_h u_i$. Let M be the matrix $M = LVB$, where $V = (I - A)^{-1}$. An element m_{ij} of this matrix indicates the expenditure of labour of type i socially necessary to reproduce one hour of labour of type j. The matrix M thus describes the reproduction of labour-power through concrete labours themselves. *Surplus labour* can therefore be expressed as

$$LVu = LV(I - A - BL)x = LV(I - A)x - LVBLx = (I - M)Lx$$

(Surplus-labour is thus a vector of concrete labours.)

Since Lx represents the total expenditure of direct labour, and MLx the expenditure of labour required to reproduce total labour-power, we have:

Proposition 1. Surplus-labour equals direct labour minus the labour necessary for the reproduction of labour-power.

Now, by means of the value-system, we move from these vector relations to quantities of abstract labour.

New-value, or the value of the net product, is

$$\lambda(I-A)x = \alpha Lx.$$

Reproduction-value, or the value of reproduction expenditures, is

$$\lambda BLx = \alpha MLx.$$

Surplus-value, or the value of the surplus product, is

$$\lambda(I-A-BL)x = \alpha(I-M)Lx.$$

This gives us:

Proposition 2. New-value (or reproduction-value, or surplus-value) is equal to the labour directly expended (or that required for reproduction, or surplus labour) as a quantity of abstract labour.

In addition:

Surplus-value = new-value − reproduction-value.

The first part of this proposition tells us the *significance of the reduction-coefficients in production*: α_i is the amount of new-value created in the production of C_i per unit of commodity and hour of labour employed. In terms of the ratio of physical magnitudes (that is, quantities of commodities and magnitudes of value), we have:

Proposition 3. A positive surplus product is always accompanied by a positive surplus-value, but the converse is generally not the case, even for a strictly self-reproductive system.

Demonstration. It is clear that if $u > 0$, then $\lambda u > 0$ for the corresponding surplus-value. (The values considered here are always positive). That the converse is not necessarily true is shown by the following counter-example. Let us supplement the coal-iron example (see chapter 4) by adding a matrix for means of reproduction:

$$B = \begin{pmatrix} 0 & \frac{1}{24} \\ \frac{1}{20} & 0 \end{pmatrix}. \text{ From } A = \begin{pmatrix} \frac{1}{2} & \frac{1}{4} \\ \frac{1}{5} & \frac{1}{2} \end{pmatrix} \text{and } L = \begin{pmatrix} 2 & 0 \\ 0 & 3 \end{pmatrix}$$

we obtain

$$I-(A + BL) = \begin{pmatrix} \frac{1}{2} & -\frac{3}{8} \\ -\frac{3}{10} & \frac{1}{2} \end{pmatrix}.$$

For an activation $x = (x_1, x_2)$, then, the surplus product $u = (u_1, u_2)$ is given by $u_1 = \frac{1}{2}x_1 - \frac{3}{8}x_2$ and $u_2 = \frac{1}{2}x_2 - \frac{3}{10} x_1$. For the activation $x = (1, 1)$, $u > 0$, and the system is therefore strictly self-reproductive. For the activation $x = (2, 1)$, $u_1 = \frac{5}{8}(> 0)$, $u_2 = -\frac{1}{10}$ (< 0), so the surplus product u is not positive. The corresponding surplus-value, however, is positive, as it is for all reduction-coefficients $\alpha \geq 0$, since $\lambda u = \frac{5}{8}\lambda_1 - \frac{1}{10}\lambda_2 > 0$, as in the coal-iron example, where $\frac{\lambda_1}{\lambda_2} \geq \frac{2}{5} > \frac{8}{50}$ for all $\alpha \geq 0$.

Proposition 3 has the following *consequence*. If a self-reproductive system is in a condition, given by the activation x, such that a positive surplus product is produced, then surplus-value is also 'healthy', in other words positive. A 'healthy' surplus-value, however, does not necessarily imply that the system is in a 'healthy' state, although it is 'healthy in and for itself', that is, self-reproductive. The system can suffer crisis despite a 'healthy' surplus-value, if insufficient means of production or of reproduction are produced.

The expression αLx depicts the net product in the form of abstract labour, as the production outcome of an expenditure of concrete labours equal to Lx. This expenditure of labour is in turn reproduced by an expenditure MLx of concrete labours. Thus, expressed in abstract labour, an expenditure of αMLx results, through production and reproduction, in an output of αLx. The *rate of surplus-value*

$$m' = \frac{\alpha Lx - \alpha MLx}{\alpha MLx} = \frac{\alpha(I-M)Lx}{\alpha MLx}$$

is then the ratio, *in terms of abstract labour*, that compares the output of production in excess of the required expenditures to the expenditures themselves. We now want to derive, using this value magnitude, an important relation concerning the special commodity labour-power, in its totality. For conventional commodities we derived, in the form of the fundamental relation between values and prices, a relation that in turn yielded the exchange curve for these conventional commodities (see chapter 5). But the fundamental relation does not hold for the special commodity labour-power (as has been noted above). We will now derive a relation that describes the exchange of the commodity labour-power—through money—for conventional commodities, one that takes account of the special character of this commodity, in particular the 'subjective element' associated with it.

In accordance with the basic model in chapter 1 and the commodity character of labour-power as described above, the entrepreneur buys means of production and labour-powers on the appropriate markets. Let w_i be the amount of money spent per hour for labour-power of type i; w_i is thus the price of an hour of labour-power of type i, which we will designate the *wage rate*, since this is what is paid for the labour-power concerned. Let w denote the n-vector of the w_i. Let x represent an appropriate activity vector; then the *total wage* will be

$$W = wLx.$$

If p is the vector of the prices p_i of conventional commodities, then the total price of the means of production $C = pAx$. Thus, $C + W$ gives the total cost the entrepreneur incurs through the purchase of means of production and labour-power. The gross product will sold for a total price of px. Since the commodities produced are owned by the owners of the means of production—the entrepreneurs—they obtain a *total profit* P equal to the difference between receipts px and costs $C + W$. Hence

$$P = px - pAx - wLx = p(I-A)x - wLx.$$

If $N = p(I-A)x$ is the price of the net product, then $N = P + W$; the net product (in prices) then goes partly to the entrepreneur as profit, and partly to the workers as wages. The *average rate of profit*, or the average ratio of profit and cost, is then

$$r = \frac{P}{C+W} = \frac{N-W}{C+W} = \frac{1-\dfrac{W}{N}}{\dfrac{C}{N}+\dfrac{W}{N}} = \frac{1-\dfrac{W}{N}}{\dfrac{1}{R}+\dfrac{W}{N}}$$

where $R = \dfrac{N}{C}$ is the *maximum* possible average rate of profit, and occurs when $W = 0$. Whereas the rate of surplus-value describes the ratio of 'output' to 'expenditure' from the standpoint of labour (more precisely: of abstract-labour), the rate of profit r describes this ratio from the standpoint of *exchange-value*, as a cost accounting of the sort entrepreneurs would make. By the definition of P, C, and W, the rate of profit r is linked in a complex manner both to the prices of commodities p and to the prices of the special commodity labour-power w. Nonetheless, on the basis of the fundamental relation, we have

$$R = \frac{p(I-A)x}{pAx} = \frac{\lambda(I-A)x}{\lambda Ax} = \frac{\alpha Lx}{\alpha LVAx}.$$

The maximum rate of profit therefore depends on values alone, which means on the reduction-coefficients α (since the production-structure and x are regarded as fixed). Once the reduction-coefficients are determined, R is also determined. It is otherwise with the magnitude $\dfrac{W}{N}$, however, which depends not only on α but also on w and p. The ratio

$$q = \frac{wLx}{pBLx}$$

between the total wage and the total reproduction-price of labour-power is an expression of the ratio in which the aggregate commodity labour-power exchanges with all other commodities. Since these commodities enter in the proportions required for reproduction, q may be termed the *reproduction index*.

Using q, we obtain

Proposition 4.

$$r = \frac{1 + m' - q}{\frac{1 + m'}{R} + q}$$

or,

$$q = (1 + m') \cdot \frac{1 - \frac{r}{R}}{1 + r}.$$

Demonstration. The fundamental relation yields

$$q = \frac{wLx}{p(I-A)x} \cdot \frac{p(I-A)x}{pBLx} = \frac{W}{N} \cdot \frac{\lambda(I-A)x}{\lambda BLx} = \frac{W}{N} \cdot \frac{\alpha Lx}{\alpha MLx} = \frac{W}{N} \cdot (1+m').$$

If $\frac{W}{N} = \frac{q}{1 + m'}$ is inserted into the equation defining r, Proposition 4 is obtained.

The first equation in Proposition 4 gives the average rate of profit as dependent on the maximum rate of profit, the rate of surplus-value, *and* the reproduction index. If we hold the magnitudes m' and R fixed in the second equation in Proposition 4 (for these depend only on the reduction-coefficients α, apart from the structure A, B, L, x), this equation will then describe the dependence of the reproduction index $q = q(r)$ on the rate of profit r. This relation may be termed the profit–reproduction-index relation, or for short the *reproduction curve*.

Of particular interest on this curve is the point given by $q = 1$ and $\bar{r} = \frac{m'}{\frac{1 + m'}{R} + 1}$. Since $\frac{1 + m'}{R} = \frac{\lambda Ax}{\lambda BLx}$, at this point $\bar{r} = \frac{\lambda(I-A-BL)x}{\lambda Ax + \lambda BLx}$ so the average rate of profit is equal to the ratio of surplus-value to the sum of the value of the means of production and the reproduction value. Since at this special point the price of the aggregate commodity labour-power equals its reproduction price, it may be termed the *reproduction point*. The form of the reproduction curve is depicted in fig. 29.

Two fundamentally different situations should be distinguished as far as the reproduction curve is concerned: first, a

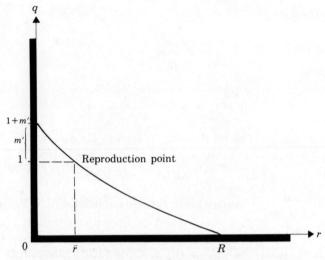

Figure 29

shift of the entire curve through changes in the structural para-
meters m', R (movement of the system itself); second, a movement of q along the curve, with m' and R fixed (movement
within the system). This distinction will play a role in *interpret-
ing the reproduction curve.*

In considering the freedom of movement of the reproduction
index relative to the reproduction-point, four cases must be
considered. They correspond to some of the situations that
arise in the literature.[8]

1.   The reproduction index moves freely; in other words, $0 \leq q$
$\leq 1 + m'$. In this case the reproduction-point plays no distinct-
ive role: q and m' can be considered together in the form $\dfrac{W}{N}$
$= \dfrac{q}{1 + m'}$ with the resultant relation

$$\frac{W}{N} = \frac{1 - \dfrac{r}{R}}{1 + r}, \quad \text{which can also be}$$

designated the profit-wage curve. No consideration of the rate
of surplus-value, or of surplus-value, is needed in this case;
what is of interest is movement along the curve more than
movement of the curve itself.

2. The reproduction index is fixed by the reproduction-point; in other words $q = 1$. In this case the fundamental relation is, so to speak, extended to the commodity labour-power, indeed globally, and the rate of profit $\bar{r}$ is determined by the value magnitudes m' and R alone. The rate of surplus-value and surplus-value are relevant magnitudes, and total surplus-value is appropriated by the entrepreneurs in the form of profits. Here shifts of the curve itself are alone of interest.

3. The reproduction index always moves above the reproduction-point; in other words $q > 1$. This case, like the following one, is a sort of mixture of cases 1 and 2. The rate of surplus-value is a relevant magnitude, and a portion of surplus-value is paid out in the form of wages.

4. The reproduction index always moves below the reproduction-point; in other words $q < 1$. In this case profit does not consist solely of surplus-value but also contains a portion of what is gained by the fact that less is paid for labour-powers than the reproduction price. On the whole, this case seems unimportant in itself.

If the reproduction price is considered simply the price of actual expenditure on consumption (given by B), the four cases can be described as follows. In order not to make any assumptions about reproduction, case 1 can be interpreted to mean that the total wage is saved. At the other extreme, case 2 occurs if no portion of the wage is saved. Case 3 means that a part but not all of the wage is saved, case 4 that 'dissaving' occurs.

A further conclusion about the reproduction curve is this: $r > 0$ if and only if $q < 1 + m'$. In case 1 this is of no consequence, for it means only that $\dfrac{W}{N} < 1$. In case 2 it tells us that $r > 0$ if and only if $m' > 0$. In case 3 it says that $m' > 0$ is a necessary condition for $r > 0$, although the converse is not necessarily true. In case 4, $r > 0$ is a necessary consequence of $m' > 0$, although not necessarily conversely.[9]

The existence of a point (q, r) that characterizes the economic relation between wage-labourers and entrepreneurs (or workers and capitalists) has two fundamental components, one more 'objective', the other more 'subjective', to wit:

—(q, r) depends on which curve the point actually lies on; in other words, on the structural conditions, determined by the rate of surplus-value and the maximum average rate of profit.

—Given these structural conditions in the form of m' and R, the actual location of (q, r) depends on the relationship of forces, the 'struggle over distribution' between wage-labourers and entrepreneurs.

The first of these components reveals that 'wages' are based on a particular kind of society, a market society, in which m' and R are significant magnitudes. This component reveals that in a market society, 'wages' constitute the price of a special commodity, one that is not produced and necessarily represents a 'subjective factor'. In case 1 the actual determination of the point (q, r) is largely left open, depending on the reproduction curve, on the struggle over distribution. In case 2, on the contrary, both $\frac{W}{N} = \frac{1}{1 + m'}$ and r are determined by the rate of surplus-value and the maximum rate of profit (which does not exclude a struggle over the structural conditions). Cases 3 and 4 are intermediate between the two extremes, the former corresponding to a stronger, the latter to a weaker, organization of wage-labourers.

The reproduction curve, then, is a prism through which the overall social relation of wages and profit can be viewed, in terms of its 'objective' (shifts of the entire curve itself) and 'subjective' (movements along the curve) components.

The results of this chapter, derived to answer the basic question formulated at its beginning, can now be summarized.

1. On the basis of abstract labour, the production of commodities can be described as the production of values, with values as inputs. The significant magnitudes are: the reproduction-value of the commodity labour-power and the surplus-value corresponding to the surplus product. These value magnitudes

depend essentially on the reduction-coefficients, which, with respect to production, correspond to the new values per unit of commodity produced and per hour of labour employed. It should be noted that although a positive surplus product always implies a positive surplus-value, the converse is not the case.

2.   A central role is played by the special character of the commodity labour-power, in particular in that it is not produced but reproduced, and in that the commodity and its owner constitute an indivisible subject. The fundamental relation for producible commodities is replaced for the commodity labour-power by the reproduction curve, which describes the dependence of the reproduction index on the average rate of profit, in both its 'objective' and 'subjective' components.

3.   The classical/contemporary labour theory of value does not offer a meaningful picture of commodity production as the production of value, since it rests not on an analysis of abstract labour but on the assumption of homogeneous labour, and therefore severs the connection between production and circulation. In the framework of abstract labour, the dogma of homogeneous labour amounts to the assumption that all reduction-coefficients are equal to 1.

7
The Standard Reduction of Labour

One essential feature of the analysis so far is that the quantities of abstract labour and the value quantities arising from it, such as commodity values, surplus-value, and so on *have not been quantitatively determined*. In other words, the reduction-coefficients, which play a central role in the concept of abstract labour as derived here and consequently in the value magnitudes obtained from it, are *variables*. The propositions formulated in the context of abstract labour so far are therefore not dependent on the reduction-coefficients' assuming any special value. (In particular, it is not assumed that the reduction-coefficients are all equal to 1; that is, homogeneous labour is not postulated.)

In this chapter we will seek to determine the reduction-coefficients quantitatively. Since the reduction-coefficients tell us the amount of value newly created in production per commodity unit and per hour of labour (see chapter 6), it is not appropriate to attempt to determine them through the reproduction of labour-power or through the wage paid for labour-power, for the value newly created in *production* is determined neither by how labour-power is reproduced nor by how it is paid for. In the fundamental relation, the reduction-coefficients are linked to the prices of commodities. So far these prices have been considered only as the price-form of commodities relative to a money-commodity (chapter 3). Let us now look at them more closely from the standpoint of production, as *prices of production*. In short, let us consider this basic question: How are the reduction-coefficients determined, and what are the consequences for prices of production, wage rates, and the reproduction curve?

Many diverse factors affect the quantitative determination of heterogeneous labour as abstract labour.[1] An answer to the basic question in its full generality would thus lead to either great imprecision or excessive tedium. We will thus concentrate on one particular type of reduction, which may be termed the *standard reduction*. Although this is but one of several ways to determine the reduction-coefficients, it is a meaningful possibility lying between the two extremes of no determination at all or one based on the dogma of homogeneous labour. It is called standard reduction because, as will be seen, it is a pendant to Sraffa's concept of a standard commodity,[2] which it resembles in being first of all a concept fashioned to investigate analytical connections. But whereas the standard commodity amounts to a proportioning of commodities that makes little economic sense, the standard reduction describes a proportioning of concrete labours against the background of the important economic concept of abstract labour.

1. The System of Prices of Production with Heterogeneous Labour

Chapter 4, section 3 dealt with costs, wages, and the rate of profit in relation to the system as a whole. We will now consider these magnitudes for sectors producing individual commodities.

Let $p = (p_1, \ldots, p_n)$ be the commodity prices per commodity unit, $w = (w_1, \ldots, w_n)$ be the hourly wage rates for the individual types of labour. The cost of production k_j of a unit of commodity C_j, produced in sector j, is thus

$$k_j = \sum_{i=1}^{n} a_{ij} p_i + l_j w_j \qquad j = 1, 2, \ldots, n.$$

The profit obtained from the sale of a unit of C_j at the price p_j is then $p_j - k_j$. The rate of profit in sector j is thus

$$r_j = \frac{p_j - k_j}{k_j} .$$

Let us now assume that changes in commodity prices and wage rates lead to a state of equilibrium in which the *rate of profit is equal for all sectors*. This assumption of a uniform rate of profit—in other words, $r_j = r$ for $j = 1, 2, \ldots, n$—can be formulated as follows: the average rate of profit $r(x)$ is independent of the activity vector x (see chapter 6, section 3). The problem of why and how a uniform rate of profit arises is one of the more difficult of political economy. But we shall follow the practice long customary in the literature on this point and make the assumption. It then follows, given the definition of production costs and the sectoral rate of profit, that the *system of prices of production with heterogeneous labour* is:

$$p_j = (1 + r) \left(\sum_{i=1}^{n} a_{ij} p_i + l_j w_j \right) \text{ for } j = 1, 2, \ldots, n;$$

or in matrix form

$$p = (1 + r)(pA + wL)$$

where r is the uniform rate of profit $(L = \text{diag } l)$.

We will not, however, adopt a second frequently made assumption, namely that there is a uniform wage rate $w_j = \bar{w}$ for $j = 1, \ldots, n$, since we want to focus on the various concrete labours. To assume a uniform wage rate is simply to mirror, at the level of prices, the assumption of homogeneous labour.[3]

In what follows it is assumed that the matrix A of the a_{ij} is both productive and, to avoid unnecessary complications, connected (irreducible). Moreover, $l_j > 0$ for $j = 1, 2, \ldots, n$. If $\varrho = \varrho(A)$ denotes the dominant eigenvalue of A, then the system has prices of production as follows (see mathematical appendix, part 1, for the subsequent argumentation):

Proposition 1.

(a)   For $r^* = \dfrac{1-\varrho}{\varrho}$, $0 < r^* < \infty$

(b) $p = (1+r) wL (I-(1+r)A)^{-1}$ for $0 \leq r < r^*$

(c) $p = (1+r)pA$ has a uniquely determined solution $p > 0$ (up to one scalar factor) and $r = r^*$.

Demonstration.

(a) Since A is productive, $0 \leq \varrho < 1$; since A is connected, $\varrho > 0$.

(b) It follows from the system of prices of production that

$$p(I-(1 + r)A) = (1 + r)wL.$$

Since $\varrho((1 + r)A) = (1 + r)\varrho(A) = \dfrac{1 + r}{1 + r^*} < 1$, it follows that $(1 + r)A$ is productive; since $(1 + r)A$ is trivially connected, $(I-(1 + r)A)^{-1}$ exists and is strictly positive (see mathematical appendix, part 1). (b) thus follows.

(c) follows from the Perron-Frobenius propositions in the mathematical appendix, part 1.

Proposition 1 tells us, according to (c) and (a), that the system of prices of production has a uniquely determined solution where $p > 0$ for the lowest possible wage rate $w_i = 0$ (up to one scalar factor), with a corresponding uniform rate of profit r^*. r^* may therefore be called the *maximum uniform rate of profit*, or for short the maximum rate of profit, so long as no confusion with the rate R from chapter 6, section 3, is possible. Part (b) of the proposition says that for all rates of profit below the maximum, unique prices of production are determined by the rate of profit and the wage rates. Taken together, (b) and (c) then imply: For any value of r, $0 \leq r \leq r^*$, and any value of w, $w \geq 0$, relative prices are uniquely determined by r and w and are positive.

A simplification occurs in the following two specific instances.

1. Where labour is regarded as homogeneous (so that $w_j = \bar{w}$ for every j), so-called prices in labour commanded $\dfrac{p}{\bar{w}}$ depend solely on the rate of profit; moreover, by eliminating prices it is possible to draw up a wage-profit relation between r and $\bar{w}$. Neither is possible with heterogeneous labour, since because of

the n unknown wage-rates $w_1, w_2, \ldots, w_n$, too many variables are involved.

2. If it is assumed that the wage rate is equal to the reproduction price for every type of labour, so that

$$w_j = \sum_{i=1}^{n} b_{ij} p_i \text{ for } j = 1, 2, \ldots, n, \text{ or } w = pB$$

then the system of prices of production becomes

$$p = (1 + r)p(A + BL).$$

If A is connected (it is sufficient that this be the case for $A + BL$), then the Perron-Frobenius propositions imply that both relative prices and the rate of profit are uniquely determined; since $w = pB$, the relative wage-rates $\dfrac{w_i}{w_j}$ are also uniquely determined.

The assumption $w = pB$ is less crucial if it is intended only to mean that the entire wage is spent on means of consumption, with no savings; but in that case B is undetermined, and we achieve little by determining p, w, and r depending on B (and, as always, on A and L). But if $w = pB$ is really intended to determine w through B, then this approach means little in a market economy, since it makes monetary magnitudes dependent on the real-wage structure B. (Cf. the discussion of the case $q = 1$ in chapter 6, section 3 and note 7 in the same chapter.)

Finally, let us illustrate the system of prices of production under heterogeneous labour by means of the coal-iron example.

The relations for the production-prices are

$$p_1 = (1 + r)(\tfrac{1}{2} p_1 + \tfrac{1}{5} p_2 + 2w_1)$$
$$p_2 = (1 + r)(\tfrac{1}{4} p_1 + \tfrac{1}{2} p_2 + 3w_2).$$

If the relative wage rate $\dfrac{w_1}{w_2}$ is denoted by u, then for relative-prices:

$$\frac{p_1}{p_2} = \frac{(1.2 + 2u) + r(1.2 - 2u)}{(3 + u) - r(3 - u)}$$

and

$$r^* = \frac{\sqrt{5} - 1}{\sqrt{5} + 1}.$$

The exchange ratio of the two commodities therefore depends on the rate of profit *and* the relative wage-rate. If labour is taken as homogeneous, so that $u = 1$, we then have *Sraffa's exchange curve*, a relation in which relative price depends solely on the rate of profit. More generally, such a curve emerges if the relative wage-rate u is held constant and the relative price treated as a function of the rate of profit alone. Two quite different types of curve emerge depending on the parameter u, according to whether u is greater or less than $\dfrac{3}{\sqrt{5}}$. These are illustrated in fig. 30.

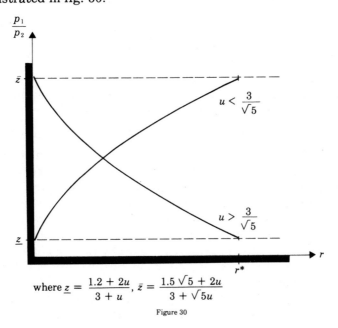

where $\underline{z} = \dfrac{1.2 + 2u}{3 + u}$, $\bar{z} = \dfrac{1.5\sqrt{5} + 2u}{3 + \sqrt{5}u}$

Figure 30

2. Definition and Properties of the Standard Reduction

We will now consider the special form of price as price of production, in terms of the fundamental relation between prices and values. This relation has already been formulated as the exchange curve (chapter 5, section 3), so we can now consider the following system.

Exchange-curve: $\dfrac{p_i}{p_j} = \dfrac{p_i}{p_j} \ (\alpha) = \dfrac{\sum\limits_{h=1}^{n} v_{hi} l_h \alpha_h}{\sum\limits_{h=1}^{n} v_{hj} l_h \alpha_h}$

$\left. \right\}$ (S)

Reproduction prices: $p = p(r, w) = (1 + r)(pA + wL)$

The variables in this system (S) are

—the reduction-coefficients $\qquad\qquad \alpha = (\alpha_1, \ldots, \alpha_n)$

—the wage rates $\qquad\qquad\qquad\qquad\ \ w = (w_1, \ldots, w_n)$

—prices $\qquad\qquad\qquad\qquad\qquad\qquad\ \ p = (p_1, \ldots, p_n)$

—the uniform rate of profit $\qquad\qquad r$.

The direct expenditures of concrete labours, $L = \operatorname{diag} l$, where $l_i > 0$, and the productive production-structure A, and hence also $V = (I - A)^{-1}$ are taken as given. If the relative reduction-coefficients $\dfrac{\alpha_h}{\alpha_g}$ (where g is arbitrary but held fixed) are determined and the rate of profit given, then the exchange curve determines relative prices, and the relations of the prices of production determine the relative wage-rates. The system (S) thus has many degrees of freedom; it is thus very much open, and has as many different solutions as there are sets of reduction-coefficients. In particular, there is no contradiction between the proportion of values to prices expressed by the exchange curve and the system of prices of production. For instance, in the coal-iron example the elimination of prices yields an equation for the three magnitudes relative reduction-coefficient, relative wage-rate and rate of profit that has solutions for many values of α and r—so there is no contradiction, but rather a gap in the determination of these magnitudes.

Now, one way to determine these magnitudes becomes possible through the following type of reduction: a vector α of the reduction-coefficients $\alpha_i > 0$ is termed *standard reduction* if

$$\frac{\lambda_i}{\alpha_i l_i} = \frac{\lambda_j}{\alpha_j l_j} \qquad \text{for } i, j, = 1, \ldots, n$$

where the λ_i are the labour-values as defined in chapter 5, section 2. The significance of the standard reduction will be discussed at length after a number of propositions about it have been derived.

The definition can be interpreted as follows. In the situation under consideration, in which several commodities are produced using several types of labour-power, a definition of the 'productivity of labour' in physical terms alone would make little sense. The expression $\dfrac{C_i}{l_i}$ could be taken intuitively as a measure of labour productivity, but this magnitude depends on *which* commodity is produced and *which* concrete labours performed. Now, the expression $\dfrac{\lambda_i}{\alpha_i l_i}$ is a dimensionless index of the productivity of labour against the background of labour as abstract labour, and indeed indicates the ratio between the total amount of direct and indirect labour required to produce an additional unit of a commodity and the particular labour required for that commodity—both expressed in terms of quantities of abstract labour. The standard reduction states that this index of labour-productivity ought to be independent of any particular commodity and concrete labour. It is thus a universal expression for the productivity of labour as abstract labour.

The existence and uniqueness of the standard reduction are ensured by

Proposition 2.

(1) A vector $\alpha > 0$ is a standard reduction if and only if there exists a number $t \geq 0$ such that

$$\alpha L A = t \cdot \alpha L.$$

(2) If A is connected, then there exists (up to one scalar factor) exactly one standard reduction. The number t in (1) is uniquely determined as $t = \varrho(A)$.

Demonstration.

(1) The equation $\alpha L A = t \cdot \alpha L$ is equivalent to $\alpha L A V = t \cdot \alpha L V,$

and since $V - AV = I$, this is equivalent to $\alpha L = (1-t)\alpha LV$. Assertion (1) follows by virtue of the value-system $\lambda = \alpha L (I-A)^{-1} = \alpha LV$.

(2) Assertion (2) follows from (1) through the Perron-Frobenius propositions in the mathematical appendix, part 1, and because α is uniquely determined by αL.

Remarks

1. For a reduction $\alpha \geq 0$, the condition $\alpha LA = t\alpha L$ in Proposition 2 holds if and only if it is the case for the value-system $\lambda = \alpha LV$ that

$$\lambda A = t \cdot \lambda.$$

The proof is as follows: $\alpha LA = t\alpha L$ is equivalent to $\alpha LAV = t\alpha LV$, and since $AV = VA$, it is also equivalent to $\lambda A = t\lambda$.

2. As is known, for a connected matrix A Sraffa's standard commodity can be characterized as the unique solution x^* of $Ax = \varrho(A)x$. In what follows, let x^* be normed such that $lx^* = 1$. α^* denotes the standard reduction uniquely determined according to Proposition 2, with the norm $\alpha^* Lx^* = 1$. x^* and α^* are *dual concepts* inasmuch as (with this norming) x^* is the unique semipositive *right eigenvector*, $\alpha^* L$ the unique semipositive *left eigenvector* of A. The term standard reduction was selected because of this parallel with the standard commodity.

In what follows let A be always connected and let x^* and α^* denote the standard commodity and standard reduction respectively (with the above norming). Let $R = R(\alpha, x) = \dfrac{\alpha Lx}{\alpha LVAx}$ be the maximum average rate of profit given an activity vector $x \geq 0$, and a vector of reduction-coefficients $\alpha \geq 0$. The following duality proposition then holds for the standard commodity and standard reduction with respect to R (which is reminiscent of the minimax theorem in game theory).

Proposition 3. (α^*, x^*) is the only point of equilibrium of $R(\alpha, x)$ (in the sense of a saddle-point); in other words,

(a)   for every $\alpha \geq 0$, $x \geq 0$,

$$R(\alpha^*, x) \leq R(\alpha^*, x^*) \leq R(\alpha, x^*)$$

and

(b) (α^*, x^*) is the only point with this property (up to the scalar multiples of α^* and x^*).

Demonstration.

(a)   For the sake of brevity, let the vector αL corresponding to a reduction α be denoted by β. By the definition of x^* and α^*, $Ax^* = \varrho x^*$ and $\beta^*A = \varrho \beta^*$, where $\varrho = \varrho(A)$. Since $\varrho(VA) = \dfrac{\varrho}{1-\varrho}$ and $VAx^* = \varrho(VA)x^*$, $\beta^*VA = \varrho(VA)\beta^*$ (mathematical appendix, part 1), and by Proposition 1, $\dfrac{\varrho}{1-\varrho} = \dfrac{1}{r^*}$, so that $VAx^* = \dfrac{1}{r^*}x^*$, $\beta^*VA = \dfrac{1}{r^*}\beta^*$. Hence

$$R(\alpha, x^*) = \frac{\beta x^*}{\beta VAx^*} = r^* \text{ for all } \alpha \geq 0 \text{ and,}$$

$$R(\alpha^*, x) = \frac{\beta^*x}{\beta^*VAx} = r^* \text{ for all } x \geq 0.$$

In particular assertion (a) follows.

(b)   Let $(\bar{\alpha}, \bar{x})$ where $\bar{\alpha} \geq 0$, $\bar{x} \geq 0$ be another point of equilibrium of R; hence $R(\bar{\alpha}, x) \leq \bar{r} \leq R(\alpha, \bar{x})$ for all $\alpha \geq 0$, $x \geq 0$, where $\bar{r} = R(\bar{\alpha}, \bar{x})$. Since (α^*, x^*) is an equilibrium-point according to (a), it follows that $\bar{r} \leq R(\alpha^*, \bar{x}) \leq R(\alpha^*, x^*) = r^*$, and similarly $r^* \leq \bar{r}$. Hence $\bar{r} = r^*$. Since $\bar{r} \leq R(\alpha, \bar{x})$ for all $\alpha \geq 0$, it follows that $\bar{r} \cdot \beta VA\bar{x} \leq \beta\bar{x}$ for all $\beta \geq 0$, hence $\bar{r} VA\bar{x} \leq \bar{x}$; since $\bar{r} = r^*$, $VA\bar{x} \leq \dfrac{1}{r^*}\bar{x}$. Since both A and VA are connected, it follows that $\bar{x} = c_1 \cdot x^*$ (for some real number c_1; see mathematical appendix). Since $R(\bar{\alpha}, x) \leq \bar{r}$ for all $x \geq 0$, it follows that $\bar{\beta}x \leq \bar{r} \cdot \bar{\beta}VAx$ for all $x \geq 0$; hence $\bar{\beta} \leq r^* \cdot \bar{\beta}VA$. Since $r^* \cdot \bar{\beta}VAx^* = r^*\bar{\beta} \cdot \dfrac{1}{r^*}x^* = \bar{\beta}x^*$ and since $x^* > 0$, so $\bar{\beta} = r^* \cdot \bar{\beta}VA$. Since VA is connected, $\bar{\beta} =$

$c_2 \cdot \beta^*$, and hence also $\bar{a} = c_2 a^*$ for some real number c_2 (mathematical appendix, part 1).

On the basis of Proposition 3, we may advance the following dual characterization of standard commodity and standard reduction with respect to R.

Conclusion. $x \geq 0$ is the standard commodity (up to one scalar factor) if and only if

$$R(a, x) \text{ is independent of } a.$$

$a \geq 0$ is the standard reduction (up to one scalar factor) if and only if

$$R(a, x) \text{ is independent of } x.$$

As far as prices are concerned, we have the following characterization of the standard reduction.

Proposition 4. Under the system (S) the following relations are mutually equivalent.

(a) $a > 0$ is the standard reduction.

(b) *Relative* wage-rates are equal to relative new values (per commodity unit and hour of labour).

(c) *Relative* prices are independent of the rate of profit.

Demonstration.

(a) and (b) are equivalent: from $p = (1 + r)(pA + wL)$ and the fundamental relation $p = t \cdot \lambda$ for some number $t > 0$, it follows that

$$wL = \frac{t}{1 + r}\lambda - t\lambda A. \text{ Because } \lambda = \lambda A + aL,$$

$$wL = taL - \frac{r}{1 + r}t\lambda. \ wL \text{ and } aL \text{ are therefore proportional}$$

if and only if aL and λ are proportional. The proportionality of aL and λ means that a is the standard reduction. The proportionality of wL and aL means that $\dfrac{w_i}{w_j} = \dfrac{a_i}{a_j}$, and hence that relative wage-rates are equal to relative reduction-coefficients, or to relative new values per commodity unit and hours of labour expended.

(a) and (c) are equivalent: (a) is equivalent to $\lambda A = \varrho \lambda$ (cf. remark 1 above). On the basis of the fundamental relation it follows from $\lambda A = \varrho \lambda$ that relative prices (not p itself) are independent of r. Conversely, if relative prices are independent of r, then there is a scalar function $f(r)$ dependent on r such that $p(r) = f(r) \cdot p(r^*)$. Since $p(r^*)A = (1 + r^*)p(r^*)$, it follows that $p(r)A = (1 + r^*)p(r)$, and the fundamental relation then yields $\lambda A = (1 + r^*)\lambda$. α is thus the standard reduction (cf. remark 1).

The next proposition characterizes the standard reduction with respect to rates of surplus-value in the various sectors. The rate of surplus-value in sector j is given by

$$e_j = \frac{\alpha_j - \sum\limits_{i=1}^{n} b_{ij}\lambda_i}{\sum\limits_{j=1}^{n} b_{ij}\lambda_i} \quad \text{for } j = 1, 2, \ldots, n.$$

These e_j are all equal to a *uniform rate of surplus-value e* if and only if

$$e \cdot \lambda B = \alpha - \lambda B, \text{ or, } (1 + e)\lambda B = \alpha.$$

Since $\lambda = \alpha L V$, we can write, using the abbreviation $M = LVB$ introduced earlier,

$$\alpha M = \frac{1}{1 + e} \alpha.$$

Thus: the sectoral rates of surplus-value have a uniform value e if and only if the vector of the reduction-coefficients α is a left eigenvector of M, to the eigenvalue $\dfrac{1}{1 + e}$. As far as the aggregate social rate of surplus-value m' is concerned (see chapter 6, section 3): m' is independent of the activity vector x if and only if all the sectoral rates of surplus-value coincide. In that case, $m' = e$. Similarly, the reproduction index $q = \dfrac{wLx}{pBLx}$ is independent of x if and only if the reproduction index is uniform for all labour-powers; in other words, if and only if $wL = t \cdot pBL$ for some number $t \geq 0$.

Proposition 5. The following statements hold for the system (S).

1. Any two of the properties 'standard reduction', 'uniform reproduction index', and 'uniform rate of surplus-value' imply the third.

2. If no portion of the wage is saved or 'dis-saved', in other words, if $w = pB$, then the standard reduction is equivalent to a uniform rate of surplus-value.

3. If no portion of the wage is saved or 'dis-saved', then under the standard reduction we have the distribution relation

$$r = \frac{e \cdot r^*}{1 + e + r^*}.$$

Demonstration. According to chapter 6, section 3 $\dfrac{W}{N} = \dfrac{q}{1 + m'}$

$= \dfrac{1 - \dfrac{r}{R}}{1 + r}$. Since there is a uniform rate of profit in the system (S), r is independent of the activity vector x. Hence $\dfrac{W}{N}$ is independent of x if and only if R is independent of x, which according to the conclusion drawn from Proposition 3 is the case if and only if there is a standard reduction. Part 1 of Proposition 5 follows. Part 2 follows in turn as a special case. Finally, part 3 follows from the global distribution relation cited at the outset, since under the assumptions that have been made, $q = 1$, $m' = e$, and $R = r^*$.

Remark

There are a number of different ways (in the form of a so-called organic composition of capital) to relate the means of production in a given sector to the labour-powers that use these means of production to manufacture commodities in that sector. For example:

(a) Ratio of the value of the means of production to new value (or to direct labour as abstract labour):

$$k_j^1 = \frac{\sum\limits_{i=1}^{n} a_{ij}\lambda_i}{l_j\alpha_j} \; .$$

(b)   Ratio of the value of the means of production to the reproduction value of the labour-power:

$$k_j^2 = \frac{\sum\limits_{i=1}^{n} a_{ij}\lambda_i}{l_j \sum\limits_{i=1}^{n} b_{ij}\lambda_i} \; .$$

(c)   Ratio of the price of the means of production to the wage:

$$k_j^3 = \frac{\sum\limits_{i=1}^{n} a_{ij}p_i}{l_j w_j} \; .$$

In general these are quite different ratios, since because of the special character of the commodity labour-power, new value, reproduction value, and the wage are quite different magnitudes. The ratios are uniform (k^1, k^2 and k^3 respectively) if:
(a') $\lambda A = k^1 \alpha L$,   (b') $\lambda A = k^2 \lambda BL$,   (c') $pA = k^3 wL$.

The relation of these conditions to the standard reduction is as follows. (a') means that the standard reduction rules. It is easy to show, using the propositions stated above, that under the system (S), (c') is also equivalent to the existence of the standard reduction. Case (b'), however, has no direct relation to the standard reduction. The definition of (b), into which the reproduction-structure B enters, corresponds to the rate of surplus-value. There is a clear relation to the standard reduction only if it is assumed that the reproduction index is uniform (in particular that $w = pB$). In that case (b') and (c') are equivalent, and (b') is therefore also equivalent to the standard reduction.

By virtue of the propositions about the standard reduction advanced so far, the following determination of the variables in the system (S) can be derived.

Proposition 6. Once the reduction-coefficients are determined through the standard reduction α^*, the system (S) has the following solution:

— for values, $\lambda = \dfrac{1 + r^*}{r^*} \cdot \alpha^* L$

— for prices, $p(r) = \bar{p}(r) \cdot \dfrac{1 + r^*}{r^*} \cdot \alpha^* L$

— for wages, $w(r) = \bar{w}(r) \cdot \alpha^*$.

In this context $\bar{p}(r)$ and $\bar{w}(r)$ are scalar functions of r for $0 \le r \le r^*$. For a given profit-rate r, $\bar{p}(r)$ and $\bar{w}(r)$ indicate the absolute level of prices and wages respectively; the following relation holds between them.

$$\frac{\bar{w}(r)}{\bar{p}(r)} = \frac{1 - \dfrac{r}{r^*}}{1 + r} \quad \text{for } 0 \le r \le r^*.$$

Demonstration. The determination of values follows directly from the definition of the standard reduction plus Proposition 2 and $r^* = \dfrac{1 - \varrho}{\varrho}$. The proposition on prices follows by virtue of the fundamental relation with a proportionality factor $\bar{p}(r)$ dependent on r. The proposition on wages follows from Proposition 4, with a proportionality factor $\bar{w}(r)$ dependent on r. Given these proportionalities, the system of prices of production $p = (1 + r)(pA + wL)$ is equivalent to

$$\bar{p}(r) \cdot \frac{1+r^*}{r^*} \cdot \alpha^* L = (1+r)(\bar{p}(r) \cdot \frac{1+r^*}{r^*} \cdot \alpha^* LA + \bar{w}(r) \cdot \alpha^* L).$$

Since α^* is the standard reduction, and since $\alpha^* L \ne 0$, because of Proposition 2 this equation is equivalent to

$$\bar{p}(r) \cdot \frac{1 + r^*}{r^*} = (1 + r)(\bar{p}(r) \cdot \frac{1}{r^*} + \bar{w}(r))$$

and hence equivalent to $\quad \dfrac{\bar{w}(r)}{\bar{p}(r)} = \dfrac{1 - \dfrac{r}{r^*}}{1 + r}$.

Remarks

1.   Under the standard reduction, λ, p, and wL are all proportional to a^*L and thus also to each other. In the light of this proportionality, the multi-sectoral system of prices of production reduces to a single macro-economic relation between the level of prices and the level of wages.

2.   This relation can be interpreted as follows: it indicates the price-level in terms of labour-commanded, $\dfrac{\bar{p}(r)}{\bar{w}(r)}$, depending on the rate of profit r. If $N(x)$ is the net product (in prices), $W(x)$ the total wage, both under the activity vector x, then under the standard reduction, $\dfrac{W(x)}{N(x)} = \dfrac{\bar{w}(r)}{\bar{p}(r)}$ for *all* x and all r. The indicated relation can thus also be read as the distribution relation

$$\frac{W(x)}{N(x)} = \frac{1 - \dfrac{r}{r^*}}{1 + r} \quad \text{for all } x \geq 0,\ 0 \leq r \leq r^*.$$

3.   Even under the standard reduction, only the *relative* ratios between the sectors are established, not the absolute magnitudes $\bar{p}(r)$ and $\bar{w}(r)$—even when the rate of profit r is given (r itself is also a variable under the standard reduction).

4.   If the relation of reproduction $w = pB$ is added to the system (S), then under the standard reduction

$$\bar{w}(r)a^* = \bar{p}(r)a^*LVB = \bar{p}(r)a^*M,$$

and hence

$$\frac{\bar{w}(r)}{\bar{p}(r)} = \frac{1}{1 + e}.$$

This does indeed express r through e (cf. Proposition 5), but is not an additional assertion about the levels $\bar{p}(r)$ and $\bar{w}(r)$. Thus: even if the standard reduction, the relation of reproduction $w = pB$, and a given uniform rate of surplus-value are assumed, the levels $\bar{p}(r)$ and $\bar{w}(r)$ remain undetermined (only their ratio is established, since the profit-rate is established).

With the aid of the exchange curve, the standard reduction can be described in the following terms. In the relation $\lambda = t \cdot \alpha L$, $(t > 0)$, which defines the standard reduction, the left side corresponds to the exchange curve. As for the right side, let us consider a relation that may be termed the *standard curve*, namely

$$\frac{p_i}{p_j}(\alpha) = \frac{\alpha_i l_i}{\alpha_j l_j} \text{ for } i, j, = 1, \ldots, n.$$

If we admit the case of a non-connected A, where several (non-proportional) standard reductions may exist, then the standard reduction (with norming) can be described thus: a standard reduction corresponds to a point at which the exchange curve and the standard curve intersect. (A point of intersection is one at which for every pair (i, j) the appropriate (i, j)-exchange-curve cuts the (i, j)-standard-curve.) With this geometric description we can look again at a few of the examples considered earlier (cf. chapter 5, section 3).

Illustration of the standard reduction

In the three examples $n = 2$. For brevity let us write $z = \frac{p_1}{p_2}$ for the exchange ratio of the two commodities and $\alpha = \frac{\alpha_1}{\alpha_2}$ for the relative reduction-coefficients of the two types of labour. In all three cases the standard curve will then have the form

$$z = \frac{\alpha_1 l_1}{\alpha_2 l_2} = \alpha \cdot \frac{l_1}{l_2}.$$

1. *Coal-iron*

The situation is represented in fig. 31. The equation for the standard curve is $z = \frac{2}{3}\alpha$; there is exactly one intersection point at $\alpha = \frac{3}{\sqrt{5}}$. In this example, then, there is exactly one (normed) standard reduction (A is connected).

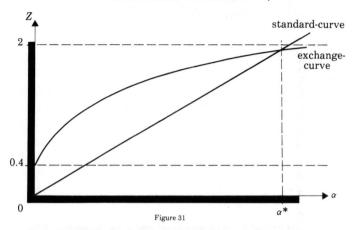

Figure 31

2. *Sraffa's beans*

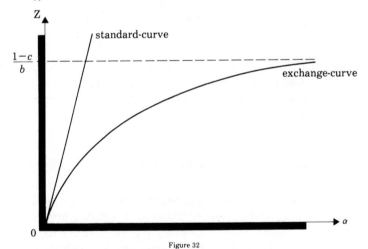

Figure 32

The situation is represented in fig. 32. The standard curve is given by $z = \dfrac{l_1}{l_2}\alpha$; apart from $\alpha = 0$, there is no intersection point of the standard curve and the exchange curve for any ratio $\dfrac{l_1}{l_2}$, since $a < c$. In this example, then, there is *no* standard reduction at all (A is not connected).

3. *Smith's deer-beaver*

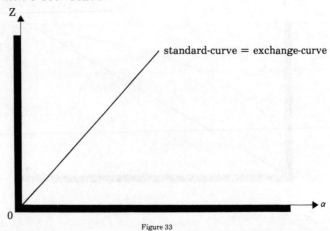

Figure 33

The situation is represented in fig. 33. The standard curve is $z = \dfrac{l_1}{l_2}\alpha$, and is therefore identical to the exchange curve. In this example, then, *every* $\alpha > 0$ corresponds to a standard reduction (A is not connected in the extreme sense). The standard reduction never serves to establish the relative ratios between deer and beaver.

3. Significance of the Standard Reduction

As has been noted, the standard reduction for individual labours is a kind of counterpart to the standard commodity for individual commodities. This duality is evident in Propositions 2 and 3, and especially in the conclusion drawn from Proposition 3. This conclusion tells us that the standard commodity is precisely distinguished by the fact that the maximum average rate of profit R is always equal to r^*, *independently* of the kind of reduction being considered. In the context of abstract labour this can be formulated somewhat differently: the whole point of the standard commodity is just exactly to deal with the kind of special situation (that is, x^*) in which the validity of the propositions (about R) in no way depends on the proportion in which one concrete labour is equated with another as abstract labour. In other words: if we look at the economic system in standard proportions (proportions appropriate to the standard commodity), then whatever view we have of abstract labour—whether we assume homogeneous labour, effect the standard reduction, or even have no view at all—the propositions about R will be unaffected. This holds not only for R but for other questions as well, like distribution. The global relation

$$\frac{W}{N} = \frac{1 - \frac{r}{R}}{1 + r}$$

(see chapter 6, section 3) yields no unique wage–profit relation between the share of wages in net product and the rate of profit, even with a uniform rate of profit r, since the variable R still depends on the type of reduction (on prices, in Sraffa's view). But precisely if the share of wages in net product is measured in terms of the standard commodity, a unique wage–profit relation of the Sraffian type emerges, since in that case $R = r^*$ regardless of the type of reduction (for Sraffa, regardless of prices; formally, Sraffa's relation is somewhat different, since he does not treat wages as advanced; in that case, as above, the share of wages in the net product as measured in the standard commodity, will be $1 - \frac{r}{r^*}$.)

Now, Sraffa considered neither abstract labour nor reduction-coefficients, but assumed homogeneous labour. His work was directed toward Ricardo's quest for an invariant standard of measurement independent of prices, and not towards Marx's concept of abstract labour. Sraffa's device of the standard commodity enabled him to disregard the problem of abstract labour and, without any loss of validity, to rest on this position of homogeneous labour. And this, of course, is possible only if the economic system is proportioned through the standard commodity. Although Sraffa did not formulate the issue in these terms, an answer to the problem of homogenizing labour of various types can also be seen in his proportioning. The other answer is that of Marx, who did not consider significant Ricardo's formulation of the problem as the quest for an invariant standard of measurement. Relying essentially on Bailey's critique of Ricardo, Marx constructed various versions of an analysis of the value-form, out of which emerged an entirely new concept in classical political economy, that of abstract labour. (In this context, the reason for the futility of Ricardo's life-long search for an invariant standard of measurement can be sought in his insistence on homogeneous labour.) The device of the standard reduction is a pendant, with respect to abstract labour as expounded in chapter 5, to the device of the standard commodity. Since, under any desired proportioning x of the economic system, the inter-relation of concrete labours as abstract labour is important, what is sought is a proportioning, within the framework of abstract labour, for which a unique wage—profit relation holds; in other words, for which $R = r^*$ regardless of the proportioning x. But in accordance with the conclusion drawn from Proposition 3, this is precisely the standard reduction of labour. Standard commodity and standard reduction are two possibilities through which the connection between commodities (to which x relates) and labours (to which α relates), highly complex in reality, can be analysed 'as in a vacuum', to use Sraffa's expression. If the economic system is considered in standard proportions, the investigation can be detached from problems of proportioning labour (that is, from α); if labour is considered in standard proportions (through the standard reduction), the investigation can be detached from problems of proportioning commodities (that is, from x). As we have seen as regards R and the distribution relation, each mode of consideration can be translated into the other by virtue of the duality of x^* and α^*. (If x and α are viewed in their interaction, Proposition 3 enables us to distinguish the pair (α^*, x^*) from all other pairs (α, x), for it is the only saddle-point on R.)[4]

Proposition 5 inaugurates a further interpretation of the standard reduction. If it is assumed that $w = pB$, then the standard reduction is equivalent to an equal rate of surplus-value for all types of labour-power. This can be interpreted: the standard reduction describes social labour uniformly as surplus-value-creating labour (in the framework of abstract labour and on the assumption that $w = pB$). And it is this feature of labour that, in accordance with $r = \dfrac{e \cdot r^*}{1 + e + r^*}$, is responsible for a positive rate of profit. As pointed out in the remark appended to Proposition 5, the standard reduction is also equivalent to the uniformity of certain proportions between expenditure of means of production and labour-powers (cases (a) and (c)). If the reproduction index of labour-power is assumed to be uniform (in particular, if $w = pB$), then the standard reduction is equivalent to a uniform ratio of the value of means of production to the reproduction-value of labour-power (case (b)). This latter ratio comes closest to Marx's familiar concept of organic composition as the ratio of the value of means of production to the 'value of the commodity labour-power'. The ratios suggested in Proposition 5, however, refer to abstract labour and are therefore formulated as dependent on the reduction-coefficients, which is not the case for the traditional concept of organic composition.[5]

The solution to the system (S) by means of the standard reduction given in Proposition 6 can be interpreted briefly as follows. The standard reduction allows the *relative* relations among commodities and labour-powers to be 'frozen', so that the *manifold* relations between sectors expressed in the system of prices of production can be reduced to a *single* macro-economic distribution relation between wages (given by $\dfrac{\bar{w}(r)}{\bar{p}(r)}$) and profit (given by r). The levels of wages, $\bar{w}(r)$, and prices, $\bar{p}(r)$, are themselves undetermined. (For a determination of the level of prices, refer to the discussion of the sum of money in chapter 3; the point will not be pursued further here).

The mere logical possibility of the standard reduction, regardless of whether it corresponds to reality, suggests a few simple conclusions in connection with various theoretical questions, in particular the so-called transformation problem.

First of all, with regard to the neo-Ricardian theory (following Sraffa). One central proposition of this theory, namely that with homogeneous labour relative prices depend on the rate of profit, no longer necessarily holds when labour is heterogeneous. This is shown by Proposition 4 combined with the existence of a standard reduction. In general, the system (S) is wide open if no standard reduction is assumed; all the more so is a pure system of prices of production with heterogeneous labour.

Second, with regard to neo-classical theory. The equality of relative wage-rates and relative new-value in accordance with Proposition 4 corresponds, in a way, to the view of labour as a factor of production rewarded according to its marginal product (new-value, in this case). But this analogy applies only with the standard reduction, and only relatively for the ratios between sectors, since in macro-economic terms,

$$\frac{W}{N} = \frac{1 - \frac{r}{r^*}}{1 + r} \, .$$

Third, with regard to Marxist theory. The transformation problem, ineluctable under the assumption of homogeneous labour, vanishes if commodity values are constructed as quantities of abstract labour as in chapter 5. In the framework given here, the *transformation problem* can be formulated as follows. Consider these assumptions:

(a) Proportionality of values and prices (meaningfully for $n \geq 2$)

(b) Uniform rate of profit, thus system of prices of production for every r where $0 \leq r \leq r^*$

} corresponds to system (S)

(c) Dogma of homogeneous labour, i.e.

$$\alpha_i = 1, \text{ and } w_i = \bar{w} \text{ for all } i = 1, \ldots, n.$$

(d) Non-trivial production-structure, i.e. $lA \neq \varrho l$.

The transformation problem consists simply in this, that assumptions (a)-(d) are not mutually compatible. It is readily apparent that this is true, since it follows from (a) and (c) that $\frac{p_i}{p_j}$ depends only on the production-structure, and thus in particular does not depend on r. In accordance with Proposition 4, then, there must be a standard reduction (this is where assumption (b) comes in). But since (c) tells us that $\alpha_i = 1$ for all i, here the standard reduction means that $lA = \varrho\, l$, which contradicts assumption (d). (A is connected; the $w_i = \bar{w}$ in (c) is not needed for this conclusion.) Traditionally, the transformation problem has been formulated not as the irreconcilability of (a)-(d), but in accordance with the traditional assumption of homogeneous labour, as follows. Is there a transformation of values into prices with property (a) and a specification of prices as prices of production in accordance with (b) (where it is sufficient that $r > 0$)? The answer, in conformity with the formulation in terms of the incompatibility of the assumptions is: no such transformation exists, except if the production-structure is trivial. But the real reason why the 'transformation' miscarries remains imperceptible here: it is the dogma of homogeneous labour. If assumption (c) is jettisoned, it is easy to see that assumptions (a), (b), and (d) become compatible. Proposition 6 shows that assumptions (a), (b), and (d) are mutually compatible *with the standard reduction*, since then the production-structure is 'almost never' trivial. (To be more accurate, with the standard reduction, the production-structure is trivial if and only if all the reduction-coefficients coincide; in other words, if, up to a norming, homogeneous labour has already been assumed.) Of course, assumptions (a), (b), and (d) are compatible over a wide range of possible reductions (see the discussion at the beginning of chapter 7, section 2). The point here, however, is that they are compatible *even* with the additional assumption of the standard reduction. (This can be seen, for instance, in the coal-iron example.)

The discussion of the transformation problem demonstrates once again how important it is to maintain a concept—indeed, an analytical concept—of abstract labour. If the quantities of abstract labour are hastily established, in particular in conformity with the dogma of homogeneous labour, further investigation will quickly be blocked—whereupon recourse to Sraffa's device of a standard commodity is required. In the case of the transformation problem, the dogma of homogeneous labour ensures that not only must we somehow effect the reduction, but the reduction problem and transformation problem are simultaneously compounded into a *twin-problem*.[6] Of course, the compatibility of assumptions (a), (b), and (d) here demonstrated, through which the edge is taken off the traditional transformation problem, does not itself mean that the proportionality of values and prices stated in (a) is correct. This proportionality has little to do with any 'transformation' and rather follows from quite a different series of steps: the construction of the concept of abstract labour through the money-relation between commodities (see chapter 5).

The standard reduction of labour and the various propositions related to it offer one possible answer to the basic question posed at the beginning of this chapter and shed some light on several other issues (such as the standard commodity and the transformation problem). But as I have already noted, the standard reduction is only one of a number of types of reduction possible in the framework erected in chapters 1 through 6. A more extensive study of the quantitative determination of quantities of abstract labour, which could consider other possible reductions, would be welcome. But further investigation of the standard reduction itself would be welcome too, dealing with possibilities not broached here: the production of one commodity using several types of labour (non-diagonal L); the establishment of sub-economies (non-connected A); fixed capital; and joint-production (non-diagonal output matrix). If the standard reduction were tested in such situations, its significance could be better assessed.[7] In particular, it could be seen whether the standard reduction is better fitted than the standard commodity to serve as the standard of measurement in theoretical investigations, a supposition suggested by the fact that the standard reduction embraces two categories significant in this respect: money and abstract labour.

Mathematical Appendix

This appendix contains the mathematical propositions about non-negative matrices and cone relations used in the text. One standard text on matrices, especially non-negative matrices, is F.R. Gantmacher, *Matrizenrechnung*, vol. 2, Berlin 1970; for a more mathematically oriented treatment of non-negative matrices see E. Seneta, *Non-negative Matrices*, London 1973. The most important propositions on the use of non-negative matrices in economics can be found in the bibliographical references in chapter 1, note 7, in particular the works of Abraham-Frois and Berrebi, Pasinetti, Gale, Nikaido, and Woods. Many essential propositions in this connection, later re-discovered, may be found in J.T. Schwartz, *Lectures on the Mathematical Method in Analytical Economics*, New York 1961. For a general overview of the use of reducible non-negative matrices in mathematical economics, see E. Brüggemann and A. Werner, *Theorie der Zerlegbarkeit nichtnegativer Matrixen und ihre Anwendungen in der mathematischen Ökonomie*, mimeo, Bremen 1978.

Most of the propositions on non-negative matrices are given with a few additional comments, but without proof; these proofs can be found in the works cited by Nikaido and Woods. To my knowledge the concept of 'degree' of connectedness $\sigma(A)$ and cone relations are not treated in the literature. The propositions on these matters are therefore given here with proofs.

Let us begin with some remarks on notation.

Sets

$m \, \varepsilon \, M$ m is an element of the set M

$M \subseteq N$ the set M is contained in the set N

$M \times N$ the set of all ordered pairs (m, n) where $m \, \varepsilon \, M, n \, \varepsilon \, N$ (Cartesian product)

Numbers

$\Re$ the set of real numbers with the usual operations of addition, multiplication, and their inverses.

$a \neq b; a < b; a \leq b$ two real numbers a and b are different; a is less than b; a is less than or equal to b.

$\min\limits_{1 \leq i \leq n} a_i, \ \max\limits_{1 \leq i \leq n} a_i$ the smallest (largest) of the real numbers $a_1, a_2, \ldots, a_n$.

$\sum\limits_{i=1}^{n} a_i$ the sum of the real numbers $a_1, a_2, \ldots, a_n$

Matrices

$x = (x_1, \ldots, x_n)$ n-vector; an element of the n-dimensional Cartesian product $\Re^n$ of $\Re$.

$A = (a_{ij})$ abbreviation for the $n \times n$ matrix $A = (a_{ij})$ $1 \leq i, j \leq n$; an element of the Cartesian product $\Re^{2n}$.

I $n \times n$ identity matrix for whose elements δ_{ij}: $\delta_{ij} = 1$ if $i = j$, $\delta_{ij} = 0$ if $i \neq j$.

$\operatorname{diag} x$ diagonal matrix D of the vector x with elements $d_{ij} = x_i$ for $i = j$, $d_{ij} = 0$ for $i \neq j$.

A' the transposed matrix of A, with elements $(a_{ij})' = a_{ji}$.

For two $n \times n$ matrices $A = (a_{ij})$, $B = (b_{ij})$, we will write

$A \leqq B$ if $a_{ij} \leq b_{ij}$ for all i and j

$A \leqq B$ $\qquad$ if $A \leq B$ and A and B are different

$A < B$ $\qquad$ if $a_{ij} < b_{ij}$ for all i and j.

An $n \times n$ matrix is termed

non-negaiive $\qquad$ if $0 \leqq A$

semi-positive $\qquad$ if $0 \leq A$

positive $\qquad$ if $0 < A$.

Analogously for an n-vector x. (0 denotes a matrix or vector each of whose elements is zero.)

Finally, let us note the following easily remembered usage: if A is an $n \times n$ matrix, and x and y are two n-vectors,

xA $\qquad$ the n-vector with the elements $\sum\limits_{i=1}^{n} x_i a_{ij}$ for $j = 1, \ldots, n$.

Ay $\qquad$ the n-vector with the elements $\sum\limits_{j=1}^{n} a_{ij} y_j$ for $i = 1, \ldots, n$.

xAy $\qquad$ the number $\sum\limits_{i,j=1}^{n} x_i a_{ij} y_j$

The expression $xIy = \sum\limits_{i=1}^{n} x_i y_i$ is abbreviated $x \cdot y$ and is called the inner product of x and y.

1.   Non-Negative Matrices

Unless otherwise stated the following matrices and vectors are $n \times n$ matrices and n-vectors.

Definition   A matrix $A \geqq 0$ is called *productive* if there exists a vector $x \geq 0$ such that $Ax < x$.

Proposition 1

(1)   A matrix $A \geqq 0$ is productive if and only if the matrix $I - A$ is

invertible and $(I-A)^{-1} \geqq 0$ holds for its inverse, the so-called Leontief inverse.

(2)   If A is productive, the Leontief inverse has the form

$$(I-A)^{-1} = \sum_{k=0}^{\infty} A^k$$

(for a proof of this proposition, see Nikaido, p. 95, or Woods, p. 7, where there is also a characterization of the productivity of A, generalized for $n \geq 2$, through the Hawkins-Simon conditions).

Remarks

1.   It follows immediately from the definition of a productive matrix that if A is productive, then so is any $p \times p$ sub-matrix $A^* = (a_{ij})_{1 < i, j < p}$ where $1 \leq p \leq n$.

2.   As is clear from Proposition 1: A is productive if and only if A' is productive. And: if A is productive, then the Leontief inverse is diagonal if and only if A is diagonal. (A matrix is called diagonal if it has the form diag x, where x is a vector).

3.   If $A \geqq 0$ is a matrix for which the sums of each of the rows or of each of the columns is less than 1, i.e.

$$\sum_{j=1}^{n} a_{ij} < 1 \text{ for all } i, \text{ or } \sum_{i=1}^{n} a_{ij} < 1 \text{ for all } j, \text{ then}$$

A is productive (the definition is fulfilled for x when $x_i = 1$ for every i). The converse, however, does not hold, as the following simple example of a productive matrix shows.

$$A = \begin{pmatrix} \dfrac{1}{2} & \dfrac{3}{4} \\ \dfrac{1}{5} & \dfrac{1}{2} \end{pmatrix}.$$

This is a general phenomenon: for a productive matrix A there will generally exist vectors $y \geq 0$ for which $Ay < y$ does *not* hold. Clearly, $Ax < x$ holds for *all* $x > 0$ if and only if A is of a very special form, namely a diagonal matrix with diagonal elements less than 1.

Definition. Let A be a non-negative $n \times n$ matrix. It is said of two indices i and j that there is a *chain from i to j* if $a_{ij} > 0$, or if there is a sequence $i_1, \ldots, i_r$ of indices such that

$$a_{ii_1} > 0, \, a_{i_1 i_2} > 0, \ldots, a_{i_r j} > 0$$

$(i, j, i_1, \ldots, i_r$ belong to the set $\{1, 2, \ldots, n\}$ of indices, and $r \geq 1$.) A is called *connected* (or irreducible) if there is a chain from every index to every other index. If this is not the case, then A is termed unconnected (or reducible).

Proposition 2. Let $A \geqq 0$ be a productive matrix and $V = (I-A)^{-1}$ the Leontief inverse of A. For every i, $v_{ii} > 0$ and for two different indices i and j, $v_{ij} > 0$ if and only if there is a chain from i to j.

Proof

(a) From proposition 1, $V = I + A + \sum\limits_{k=1}^{\infty} A^{k+1}$, for the elements of the matrix, thus

$$v_{ij} = \delta_{ij} + a_{ij} + \sum_{k=1}^{\infty} a_{ij}^{(k+1)} \text{ for } i, j = 1, 2, \ldots, n.$$

(b) From the definition of matrix multiplication it follows by complete induction on k that

An element $a_{ij}^{(k+1)}$ of the $(k+1)$-th power A^{k+1} of A has the form

$$a_{ij}^{(k+1)} = \sum_{(i_1, i_2, \ldots, i_k) \, \varepsilon \, I^k} a_{ii_1} \cdot a_{i_1 i_2} \ldots a_{i_k j} \text{ for } k \geq 1$$

where the summation goes over all k-tuples of the k-dimensional Cartesian product I^k of the set of indices $I = \{1, 2, \ldots, n\}$. Proposition 2 follows from (a) and (b) by the definition of a chain.

From this proposition there follows immediately

Corollary. Let $A \geqq 0$ be a productive matrix. The Leontief inverse of A is positive $(V > 0)$ if and only if A is connected. (Cf. Nikaido, p. 107, and Woods, p. 10.)

Remark. A positive matrix is always connected. But the matrix

$$\begin{pmatrix} 0 & 1 \\ 1 & 0 \end{pmatrix}$$

is also connected, while

$$\begin{pmatrix} 1 & 0 \\ 0 & 1 \end{pmatrix}$$

is not.

Definition. If for a matrix A there exist a non-zero vector x and a number t such that

$$Ax = tx$$

then t is called an *eigenvalue* of A with *eigenvector x*.

A number of special propositions about eigenvalues and eigenvectors hold for non-negative matrices, known for short as *Perron-Frobenius* propositions after their discoverers, O. Perron and F.G. Frobenius.

Proposition 3. For a matrix $A \geq 0$ there exists a largest non-negative eigenvalue $\varrho(A) \geq 0$, with a semi-positive eigenvector $x \geq 0$. (There are a number of proofs of this proposition; see Woods, p. 18 ff., p. 63, and Nikaido, pp. 100 ff.)

Definition. For a matrix $A \geq 0$ the largest non-negative eigenvalue $\varrho(A)$ is called the Perron-Frobenius eigenvalue, or for short, the *dominant eigenvalue*.

Remarks. Let A be a matrix $A \geq 0$.

1. As is immediately apparent, $\varrho(tA) = t \cdot \varrho(A)$ for every number $t \geq 0$. From the general fact that eigenvalues are the roots of the characteristic polynomial of a matrix, it follows that

$\varrho(A') = \varrho(A)$ (cf. Nikaido, p. 103).

2. Let A be productive, x a vector, t a number $\neq 1$; then $Ax = tx$ is equivalent to $(I-A)^{-1} Ax = \frac{t}{1-t} x$. It then follows in particular that

$$\varrho((I-A)^{-1}A) = \frac{\varrho(A)}{1-\varrho(A)}$$

3. A is productive if and only if $\varrho(A) < 1$. (For a proof see Nikaido, p. 102.)

For connected matrices there is a stronger proposition.

Proposition 4. Let $A \geq 0$ be a connected matrix.

(1) $\varrho(A) > 0$ with an eigenvector $x > 0$.

(2) If $Ay \leq \varrho(A)y$ for a vector y, then there is a real number t such that $y = t \cdot x$. (For proof see Nikaido, p. 107, Woods, p. 23.)

Remarks

1. $\varrho(A) = 0$ can actually occur for a non-connected semi-positive matrix A, as the following example (of a productive matrix) shows:

$$A = \begin{pmatrix} 0 & \frac{1}{2} & \frac{1}{3} \\ 0 & 0 & \frac{1}{4} \\ 0 & 0 & 0 \end{pmatrix}.$$

In this example $A^3 = 0$. In general: $\varrho(A) = 0$ if and only if for some $k \geq 1$, $A^k = 0$ (see Nikaido, p. 103).

2. If A is productive and connected and V is the Leontief inverse, then VA is also connected, since by Proposition 1

$$VA = (I-A)^{-1}A = A + A^2 + \ldots \geqq A.$$

If A is a connected matrix, then by Proposition 4, $\varrho(A) > 0$; the positivity of the dominant eigenvalue, however, is not characteristic of the property of being 'connected', as shown by the case of the identity matrix I, which is not connected but for which $\varrho(I) = 1 > 0$. Such a characterization is possible through the following number $\sigma(A)$.

Definition. For a productive matrix $A \geq 0$, $\sigma(A)$ denotes the following number

$$\sigma(A) = \inf_{\substack{x \geq 0 \\ Ax \leq x}} \frac{\min\limits_{1 \leq i \leq n} x_i}{\max\limits_{1 \leq i \leq n} x_i}$$

It follows immediately from this definition that $\sigma(A)$ is a number such that $0 \leq \sigma(A) \leq 1$.

Lemma. If $A \geq 0$ is productive and V is the Leontief inverse of A, then

$$\sigma(A) = \min_{i,j,h \, \varepsilon \, I} \frac{v_{jh}}{v_{ih}}, \text{ where } I = \{1, 2, \ldots, n\}$$

(with the convention: $\dfrac{t}{0} = +\infty$ for $t \geq 0$)

Proof. It follows from Proposition 1 that

$$\{x \geq 0 \mid Ax \leq x\} = \{Vy \mid y \geq 0\}, \text{ since:}$$

If $x \geq 0$ and $Ax \leq x$, then $y = x - Ax \geq 0$ and $x = (I-A)^{-1}y = Vy$; since $x \geq 0$, $y \geq 0$ too. If $x = Vy$ and $y \geq 0$, then $x \geq 0$ and $(I-A)x = y \geq 0$, thus $Ax \leq x$.

It then follows from the definition of $\sigma(A)$ that

$$\sigma(A) = \inf_{y \geq 0} \frac{\min\limits_{i \, \varepsilon \, I} \sum\limits_{j=1}^{n} v_{ij} y_j}{\max\limits_{i \, \varepsilon \, I} \sum\limits_{j=1}^{n} v_{ij} y_j} \qquad (*)$$

If $\bar{y} = (\delta_{1h}, \delta_{2h}, \ldots, \delta_{nh})$ for $h \, \varepsilon \, I$, then $\bar{y} \geq 0$ and it follows in particular that

$$\sigma(A) \le \frac{\min\limits_{i \,\varepsilon\, I} \; v_{ih}}{\max\limits_{i \,\varepsilon\, I} \; v_{ih}} \le \frac{v_{jh}}{v_{ih}}.$$

Since this holds for any indices i, j, h, in I, it follows that

$$\sigma(A) \le \min\limits_{i, j, h \,\varepsilon\, I} \frac{v_{jh}}{v_{ih}} \, .$$

For the converse inequality, let a be the minimum of all numbers $\dfrac{v_{jh}}{v_{ih}}$ where $i, j, h \,\varepsilon\, I$. Then $a \cdot v_{ih} \le v_{jh}$, thus $a \cdot \sum\limits_{h=1}^{n} v_{ih} \cdot y_h \le \sum\limits_{h=1}^{n} v_{jh} \cdot y_h$ for all $y \ge 0$, and all $i, j, \varepsilon\, I$. Hence

$$a \cdot \max\limits_{i \,\varepsilon\, I} \sum\limits_{h=1}^{n} v_{ih} y_h \le \min\limits_{j \,\varepsilon\, I} \sum\limits_{h=1}^{n} v_{jh} y_h \text{ for all } y \ge 0.$$

It then follows from (*) that $a \le \sigma(A)$ and the lemma is proved.

With the aid of this lemma we deduce

Proposition 5.   Let $A \ge 0$ be a productive matrix.

(1) $\sigma(A) > 0$ if and only if A is connected.

(2) $\sigma(A) = 1$ if and only if A is a 1×1 matrix (whose only element is less than 1).

Proof

(1)   On the basis of the lemma, $\sigma(A) > 0$ if and only if V contains positive elements only (as the inverse of a matrix, V has no column h consisting solely of zeros). According to the corollary to Proposition 2, this in turn is the case if and only if A is connected.

(2)   Let A be a non-negative and productive 1×1 matrix. The matrix consists of just one element, a, for which $0 \le a < 1$. A semi-positive 1-vector x such that $Ax \le x$ is any real number $x > 0$, and thus by definition of $\sigma(A)$

$$\sigma(A) = \inf_{x > 0} \frac{x}{x} = 1.$$

Conversely, let A be a non-negative $n \times n$ matrix such that $\sigma(A) = 1$. It follows by virtue of the lemma that $1 \le \frac{v_{jh}}{v_{ih}}$ for all $i, j, h \, \varepsilon \, I$, hence that $v_{ih} = v_{jh}$ for all $i, j, h \, \varepsilon \, I$.

Since $V(I-A) = I$, it follows that for all $i, j, h \, \varepsilon \, I$

$$\delta_{ik} = \sum_{h=1}^{n} v_{ih}(\delta_{hk} - a_{hk}) = \sum_{h=1}^{n} v_{jh}(\delta_{hk} - a_{hk}) = \delta_{jk}.$$

Thus $\delta_{ik} = \delta_{jk}$ for all $i, j, k \, \varepsilon \, I$, and in particular $\delta_{ij} = \delta_{jj} = 1$ for all $i, j \, \varepsilon \, I$. Since $\delta_{ij} = 0$ for $i \ne j$, I contains no two differing indices, which means that $n = 1$. This proves Proposition 5.

Remarks on the magnitude $\sigma(A)$

1. In a certain sense, $\sigma(A)$ measures the degree to which a matrix is connected. The smallest value for $\sigma(A)$, namely 0, occurs if and only if A is not connected; the largest, namely 1, occurs if and only if the matrix shrinks to a single number and is therefore 'very strongly' connected.

2. In general $\sigma(A') \ne \sigma(A)$, as the following example shows:

$$A = \begin{pmatrix} 0 & \frac{1}{5} \\ \frac{1}{2} & \frac{1}{2} \end{pmatrix} \quad \text{is non-negative and productive.}$$

$$V = \begin{pmatrix} \frac{5}{2} & \frac{5}{4} \\ 1 & \frac{5}{2} \end{pmatrix}.$$

It follows that $\sigma(A) = \frac{1}{5}$, $\sigma(A') = \frac{2}{5}$; hence $\sigma(A') \ne \sigma(A)$.

3. For the extreme values 1 and 0 of $\sigma(A)$, however:

$$\sigma(A') = 0 \text{ if and only if } \sigma(A) = 0,$$

$$\sigma(A') = 1 \text{ if and only if } \sigma(A) = 1.$$

This follows immediately from Proposition 5, together with the corollary to Proposition 2 and Remark 2 to Proposition 1.

2. Cone Relations

First, some definitions.

Definition. If M is a set, then a subset $R \subseteq M \times M$ is called a (binary) *relation* on M. If m, $n \in M$, then $(m, n) \in R$ can also be written $m \, R \, n$. A relation R on M is termed

reflexive if for all $m \in M$, $m \, R \, m$.

symmetric if it follows from $m \, R \, n$ that $n \, R \, m$.

transitive if it follows from $m \, R \, p$ and $p \, R \, n$ that $m \, R \, n$.

A reflexive, symmetric, and transitive relation is called an *equivalence relation.*

Definition. A subset $M \subseteq \Re^n$ is called a cone (in 0), if for every $m \in M$ and every number $\lambda \geq 0$, $\lambda \cdot m \in M$. A cone is called a *convex cone* if $m \in M$ and $n \in M$ imply $m + n \in M$.

Definition. Let M be a cone and R a relation on M. R is called

non-trivial if $m \, R \, 0$ or $0 \, R \, m$ holds only for $m = 0$.

homogeneous if $m \, R \, n$ and $\lambda \geq 0$ imply $\lambda m \, R \, \lambda n$.

complete if for any two non-zero elements, m, n of M there exist numbers λ, $\mu > 0$ such that $\lambda m \, R \, \mu n$.

one-one if $\lambda m \, R \, n$ and $\mu m \, R \, n$, where λ, $\mu > 0$, imply $\lambda = \mu$.

A reflexive relation on a cone that is non-trivial, homogeneous, complete, and one-one is called a *cone relation.* If M is a convex cone, a relation R on M is termed *monotonic* if for $m, n, x, y \in M$ it is the case that: if $x \, R \, y$ then $m \, R \, n$ if and only if $(m + x) \, R \, (n + y)$.

Remarks

1. It follows directly from the definition that for a cone relation

R on a cone M: to the non-zero elements m, n ε M there exists exactly one number $z(m, n) > 0$ such that m R $z(m, n) \cdot n$; and for every m ε M, $z(m, m) = 1$.

2.   If R is a cone relation on a cone M, and a is an element of M, then the following relation R_a is termed the *relation induced* by a: For m, n ε M, m R_a n if and only if there exists a number $\lambda > 0$ such that m R λa and n R λa. As is easily checked, the relations induced by a cone relation are themselves cone relations, and are indeed equivalence relations.

3.   If a symmetric and reflexive relation R on a convex cone is monotonic, then it is an equivalence relation. Since: from m R p and p R n it follows by virtue of monotonicity that $(m + p)$ R $(n + p)$; since R is reflexive, it follows from p R p and monotonicity that m R n. R is therefore transitive, and since it is already assumed that it is symmetric, it is an equivalence relation.

   The next proposition relates to the particular convex cone $\mathfrak{R}_+^n = \{x \; \varepsilon \mathfrak{R}^n \mid x \geq 0\}$; in what follows e_i denotes the i-th unit vector in $\mathfrak{R}^n$, i.e. the vector

$e_i = (\delta_{1i}, \delta_{2i}, \ldots, \delta_{ni})$; a vector x ε $\mathfrak{R}^n$

with the components x_i for $i = 1, \ldots, n$ thus has the form

$$x = \sum_{i=1}^{n} x_i e_i.$$

Proposition 6.   Let Θ be a non-trivial, homogeneous, monotonic, and symmetric relation on the cone $\mathfrak{R}_+^n$ with the following property:

   There exist linearly independent vectors $v_1, v_2, \ldots, v_n$ ε $\mathfrak{R}_+^n$ such that

$v_i \; \Theta \; v_i$ for every $i = 1, \ldots, n$.

for every ordered pair (v_i, v_j) there exists a number $s > 0$ such that $v_i \; \Theta \; s \cdot v_j$.

It then follows that:

(1) Θ is an equivalence relation.

(2) Θ is a cone relation.

(3) For any two vectors x, y, $\varepsilon \, \Re^n$ with $x \geq 0$ and $y \geq 0$, there exists a uniquely determined number $z(x, y) > 0$ such that $x \, \Theta \, z(x, y) \cdot y$.

If $\alpha_{ij} = z(e_i, e_j)$ for $i, j = 1, \ldots, n$, then

$$z(x, y) = \frac{\sum\limits_{i=1}^{n} \alpha_{ij} x_i}{\sum\limits_{i=1}^{n} \alpha_{ij} y_i} \quad \text{for every } j = 1, \ldots, n.$$

(4) For all x, $y \, \varepsilon \, \Re^n$ with $x \geq 0$, $y \geq 0$,

$$\min_{1 \leq i \leq n} \frac{x_i}{y_i} \leq z(x, y) \leq \max_{1 \leq i \leq n} \frac{x_i}{y_i}.$$

Proof. Let I be the set of indices $I = \{1, \ldots, n\}$. In what follows all summations are over I.

1. We first show that for every $j \, \varepsilon \, I$ there exists an $a_j > 0$ such that $e_j \, \Theta \, a_j \cdot v_1$ (*). Let any index $j \, \varepsilon \, I$ be *chosen and fixed*. Since the v_i, $i \, \varepsilon \, I$, are linearly independent, there exist real numbers r_k, $k \, \varepsilon \, I$, such that $e_j = \sum\limits_k r_k v_k$. Let $r_k^+ = \max(r_k, 0)$ and $r_k^- = -\min(r_k, 0)$. Then r_k^+, $r_k^- \geq 0$ and $r_k = r_k^+ - r_k^-$. Hence, $e_j = \sum\limits_k r_k^+ v_k - \sum\limits_k r_k^- v_k$.

By assumption there exist numbers $s_k > 0$ such that $v_k \, \Theta \, s_k v_1$ for $k \, \varepsilon \, I$. Since Θ is homogeneous and monotonic, it follows that

$$\left(\sum\limits_k r_k^+ v_k \right) \Theta \left(\sum\limits_k r_k^+ s_k \right) v_1 \text{ and } \left(\sum\limits_k r_k^- v_k \right) \Theta \left(\sum\limits_k r_k^- s_k \right) v_1,$$

from which it follows, since Θ is symmetric and monotonic, that

$$\left[\sum\limits_k r_k^+ v_k + \left(\sum\limits_k r_k^- s_k \right) v_1 \right] \Theta \left[\left(\sum\limits_k r_k^+ s_k \right) v_1 + \sum\limits_k r_k^- v_k \right];$$

on the basis of the expression for e_j, we have

$$\left[e_j + \sum\limits_k r_k^- v_k + \left(\sum\limits_k r_k^- s_k \right) v_1 \right] \Theta \left[\left(\sum\limits_k r_k^+ s_k \right) v_1 + \sum\limits_k r_k^- v_k \right].$$

Since $v_k \ominus v_k$ for every $k \, \varepsilon \, I$, it follows by virtue of the homogeneity and monotonicity of $\ominus$ that

$$(\sum_k r_k^- v_k) \ominus (\sum_k r_k^- v_k).$$

Finally, by means of this relation it follows from the monotonicity of $\ominus$ that

$$[e_j + (\sum_k r_k^- s_k) v_1] \ominus (\sum_k r_k^+ s_k) v_1. \qquad (**)$$

If it were the case that

$\sum_k r_k^+ s_k \leq \sum_k r_k^- s_k$, then since $v_1 \ominus v_1$

and since $\ominus$ is homogeneous and monotonic, it would follow that

$$[e_j + (\sum_k r_k^- s_k - \sum_k r_k^+ s_k) v_1] \ominus 0.$$

Since $\ominus$ is non-trivial, it would therefore be the case that $e_j = t \cdot v_1$ where $t = \sum_k (r_k^+ - r_k^-) s_k \leq 0$. Since $e_j \neq 0$, t cannot be zero, and since $v_1, e_j \, \varepsilon \, \mathfrak{R}_+^n$, it cannot be the case that $t < 0$.

This case is thus not possible, and therefore

$$\sum_k r_k^- s_k < \sum_k r_k^+ s_k.$$

Similarly, since $v_1 \ominus v_1$ and since $\ominus$ is homogeneous and monotonic, it follows from (**) that

$$e_j \ominus (\sum_k r_k^+ s_k - \sum_k r_k^- s_k) v_1.$$

Hence

$$e_j \ominus a_j \cdot v_1 \text{ where } a_j = \sum_k r_k s_k > 0$$

Since $j \, \varepsilon \, I$ was selected arbitrarily, (*) is proved.

Now, let $x, y \, \varepsilon \, \mathfrak{R}^n$ where $x \geq 0$, $y \geq 0$, $x = \sum_i x_i e_i$, $y = \sum_i y_i e_i$. By virtue of the homogeneity and monotonicity of Θ it follows from (*) that

$$(\sum_i x_i e_i)\,\Theta\,(\sum_i x_i a_i)v_1,$$

and thus

$$x\,\Theta\,(\sum_i x_i a_i)\,v_1$$

and likewise

$$y\,\Theta\,(\sum_i y_i a_i)v_1.$$

Since $a_i > 0$ for $i\,\varepsilon\,I$, and $x \geq 0$, so $\sum_i x_i a_i > 0$, and likewise $\sum_i y_i a_i > 0$.

It therefore follows from the homogeneity and symmetry of Θ that

$$\frac{1}{\sum_i x_i a_i}\,x\,\Theta\,v_1 \quad\text{and}\quad v_1\,\Theta\,\frac{1}{\sum_i y_i a_i}\,y$$

and from monotonicity that

$$(v_1 + \frac{1}{\sum_i x_i a_i}\,x)\,\Theta\,(v_1 + \frac{1}{\sum_i y_i a_i}\,y).$$

Since $v_1\,\Theta\,v_1$, it finally follows from homogeneity and monotonicity that

$$x\,\Theta\,a\cdot y \quad\text{where}\quad a = \frac{\sum_i x_i a_i}{\sum_i y_i a_i} > 0. \qquad (***)$$

Θ is therefore complete. Specifically, if $x = y$, then $a = 1$, and since $x\,\Theta\,x$, Θ is reflexive (since $v_1\,\Theta\,v_1$ and Θ is homogeneous, it trivially follows that $0\,\Theta\,0$). Since Θ is therefore symmetric, monotonic, and reflexive, it follows from Remark 3 to the definitions above that Θ is an equivalence relation.

2. To show that Θ is a cone relation, it remains only to show

that Θ is one-one. To do so let $\lambda x \ \Theta \ y$ and $\mu x \ \Theta \ y$, for some numbers $\lambda, \mu > 0$ and $x, y \ \varepsilon \ \mathfrak{R}_+^n$; since Θ is non-trivial, $x \geq 0$ and $y \geq 0$. Since Θ is symmetric and monotonic, $(\lambda x + y) \ \Theta \ (\mu x + y)$. Since (1) tells us that Θ is reflexive, $y \ \Theta \ y$, and it therefore follows from monotonicity that $\lambda x \ \Theta \ \mu x$. Let $\lambda \leq \mu$; it follows from monotonicity and reflexivity that $0 \ \Theta \ (\mu-\lambda)y$, and hence, since Θ is non-trivial, $(\mu-\lambda)x = 0$, and since $x \neq 0$, μ and λ must be equal. It similarly follows that $\mu = \lambda$ if $\lambda \geq \mu$. Θ is therefore one-one, and thus a cone relation.

3. Since Θ is a cone relation, it follows from Remark 1 to the definitions above that: For $x, y \ \varepsilon \ \mathfrak{R}_+^n$ where $x \geq 0$, $y \geq 0$, there exists a uniquely determined number $z(x, y)$ such that $x \ \Theta \ z(x, y)y$. Because of (***)

$$z(x, y) = \frac{\sum\limits_i x_i a_i}{\sum\limits_i y_i a_i} \ . \text{ It follows in particular that}$$

$\alpha_{ij} = z(e_i, e_j) = \dfrac{a_i}{a_j}$, and hence that

$$z(x, y) = \frac{\sum\limits_i \alpha_{ij} x_i}{\sum\limits_i \alpha_{ij} y_i} \quad \text{for every } j = 1, \ldots, n.$$

4. For all $i \ \varepsilon \ I$

$$(\min_k \frac{x_k}{y_k}) \cdot y_i \leq x_i \leq y_i \cdot \max_k \frac{x_k}{y_k} \ .$$

Through multiplication with $\alpha_{ij} > 0$ and summation over i, (4) follows from (3).

Remark

A mapping $f \colon \mathfrak{R}_+^n \to \mathfrak{R}$ is termed homogeneous if $f(\lambda x) = \lambda f(x)$ for all $x \ \varepsilon \ \mathfrak{R}_+^n$ and all $\lambda \geq 0$; f is termed positive if $f(x) > 0$ for all $x \ \varepsilon \ \mathfrak{R}_+^n, x \neq 0$; f is termed additive if $f(x + y) = f(x) + f(y)$ for all $x, y \ \varepsilon \ \mathfrak{R}_+^n$. If Θ is a relation on $\mathfrak{R}_+^n$ and f is a mapping $f \colon \mathfrak{R}_+^n \to \mathfrak{R}$, it is said that f represents Θ if for all x, $y \,\varepsilon\, \mathcal{R}^n_+$, $x \,\Theta\, y$ is equivalent to $f(x) = f(y)$.

1.   It therefore follows from Proposition 6 that a relation with the properties stated in that proposition can be represented by a homogeneous, positive, additive function f. The function $f(x)$ $= \sum\limits_i \alpha_{ij} x_i$ is such a representation for any arbitrary $j \,\varepsilon\, I$; f is trivially homogeneous, positive, and additive, from part (3) of Proposition 6 it follows that $x \,\Theta\, y$ is equivalent to $z(x, y) = 1$, and hence that f is a representation of Θ.

2.   The assumptions about Θ made in Proposition 6, however, are not only sufficient for Θ to be represented by a homogeneous, positive, additive function, but are also necessary. Let Θ be a relation on $\mathcal{R}^n_+$ represented by a homogeneous, positive, and additive function $f: \mathcal{R}^n_+ \to \mathcal{R}$. Since Θ is represented by f, Θ is symmetric (indeed, it is an equivalence relation). Since f is positive, Θ is non-trivial. Since f is homogeneous, Θ is homogeneous. If $f(x) = f(y)$, then by virtue of the additivity of f, $f(m) = f(n)$ is equivalent to $f(m + x) = f(n + y)$, and Θ is therefore monotonic. Finally, the last demand placed on Θ in Proposition 6 is also fulfilled for every set of n linearly independent vectors in $\mathcal{R}^n_+$, in particular $v_i = e_i$ for $i \,\varepsilon\, I$; for since Θ is represented by f, Θ is reflexive, and since for $x \geq 0$ and $y \geq 0$, $f(\frac{1}{f(x)} \cdot x) = f(\frac{1}{f(y)} \cdot y)$, f is indeed complete.

References

Chapter 1

1. Antoine Cournot, *Recherches sur les principes mathématiques de la théorie des richesses* (1838); Karl Marx, *Capital* Volume 1, Penguin Books in association with *New Left Review*, Harmondsworth 1976, chapter 1.

2. See, Paul Einzig, *Primitive Money, In Its Ethnological, Historical and Economic Aspects*, 2nd edn, Oxford 1966. Maurice Godelier, *Rationality and Irrationality in Economics*, London 1972. Marshall Sahlins, *Stone Age Economics*, London 1974. 'Primitive' societies are so complex and diverse that it would be a mistake to interpret them as different stages in a linear development towards a 'higher' form of society (market, or socialist?). Sahlins, for example, objects to 'businesslike interpretations of primitive economies and societies' (*Stone Age Economics*, p. xi).

3. This notion of distribution is much wider than the idea of income-distribution usually encountered in economic theory. It is oriented toward the very broad concept of distribution employed by Godelier to describe how a society regulates the distribution of goods to various productive uses and to various individuals or groups of individuals (*Rationality and Irrationality*, pp. 311 ff.).

4. Following Polanyi, we may distinguish three basic modes of distribution within the variety of actual distribution systems: reciprocity, redistribution, and exchange. See the contributions by Polanyi, H. Codere, and the introduction by Schlicht, in E. Schlicht, *Einführung in die Verteilungstheorie*, Hamburg 1975. See also *Rationality and Irrationality*, pp. 311 ff. and *Stone Age Economics*, pp. 185 ff.

5. On law, see Evgeny Pashukanis, *Law and Marxism*, London 1978. For a more precise specification of law using Arrow's impossibility theorem, see Ulrich Krause, *Individuum, Recht und Gesellschaft* (mimeo), Bremen 1975.

6. The expressions (3), (3'), and (3'') are reminiscent of the basic formula of control theory, with P as the regulated member and E (or D) as regulator. But $\bar{L}$ and $\bar{Y}$ (labour and commodities) are not additive. These expressions are intended to be illustrative and should not be interpreted to imply a cybernetic analysis of economic linkages.

7. Representations of production as in (1') have been customary for some time in economics. The extensive literature on the subject, from many sources, deals with a variety of associated sets of problems. The main groupings, among which there are many inter-connections, are as follows.

First, studies in connection with Piero Sraffa, *Production of Commodities by Means of Commodities*, Cambridge 1960. More recent works, which themselves provide additional references, are: G. Abraham-Frois and E. Berrebi, *Théorie de la Valeur, des Prix et de l'Accumulation*, Paris 1976; H.D. Kurz, *Zur neoricardianischen Theorie des Allgemeinen Gleichgewichts der Produktion und Zirkulation*, Berlin 1977; L.L. Pasinetti, *Lectures on the Theory of Production*, London 1977; A. Roncaglia, *Sraffa and the Theory of Prices*, New York 1978. Specifically on joint production see the detailed study by E. Schefold, *Mr Sraffa on Joint Production*, Basle 1971. Also G. Hodgson, *The Effects of Joint Production and Fixed Capital in Linear Economic Analysis* (mimeo), Manchester 1974; A. van Schaik, *Reproduction and Fixed Capital*, Tilburg 1976; M. Cogoy, *Wertstruktur und Preisstruktur, Die Bedeutung der linearen Produktionstheorie für die Kritik der politischen Ökonomie*, Frankfurt 1977.

Second, mathematically oriented treatments of Marx's theory: A. Bródy, *Proportions, Prices and Planning. A Mathematical Restatement of the Labor Theory of Value*, Amsterdam 1970; M. Morishima, *Marx's Economics. A Dual Theory of Value and Growth*, Cambridge 1973; G. Maarek, *Introduction au Capital de Karl Marx. Un Essai de Formalisation*, Paris 1975; E. Wolfstetter, *Wert, Profitrate und Beschäftigung, Aspekte der Marxschen und der klassischen Wirtschaftstheorie*, Frankfurt 1977; W. Semmler, *Zur Theorie der Reproduktion und Akkumulation*, Berlin 1977; I. Steedman, *Marx after Sraffa*, London 1977.

Third, activity analysis and linear economic models: R. Dorfman, P.A. Samuelson, and R.M. Solow, *Linear Programming and Economic Analysis*, New York 1958; D. Gale, *The Theory of Linear Economic Models*, New York 1960; H. Nikaido, *Convex Structures and Economic Theory*, New York 1968; K. Hildenbrand and W. Hildenbrand, *Lineare ökonomische Modelle*, Berlin 1975; O. Morgenstern and G.L. Thompson, *Mathematical Theory of Expanding and Contracting Economies*, Lexington 1976; J.E. Woods, *Mathematical Economics. Topics in Multi-sectoral Economics*, London 1978. See, too, the unique modelling in N. Georgescu-Roegen, *The Entropy Law and the Economic Process*, Cambridge, Mass. 1971, pp. 211, et. seq.

Most of these contributions are based on the assumption of homogeneous labour. See, for example, Sraffa, *Production of Commodities*, Paragraph 10, p. 10. For a number of approaches that seek to include differing types of labour, see Ulrich Krause, *Elemente einer multisektoralen Analyse der Arbeit, Diskussionsbeiträge zur Politischen Ökonomie*, no. 5, Bremen 1978.

In most of the cited literature, exchange is formulated in connection with production using relative prices. This differs from the formulation of exchange in (2′), where exchange ratios are not necessarily derived from relative prices. For example, the possible exchange ratios in (2′) correspond to those 'which spring directly from the methods of production' (Sraffa, *Production of Commodities*, Paragraph 1) only when $n = 2$, in other words, when an exchange is necessarily direct. (See the subsequent discussion of value- and price-form). Accordingly, the formulation of the connection between production and exchange in (3′) differs from the usual Sraffian postulation of a system of physical quantities and a price system (to which a system of values related to labour times is frequently appended).

Property relations and their connection to the production structure have been almost completely ignored in the models set out above. On the 'institutional context', see J.R. Commons, *Legal Foundations of Capitalism*, Madison 1968; O.E. Williamson, *Markets and Hierarchies: Analysis and Antitrust Implications*, New York 1975. (See chapter 7 below on the particular commodity of labour-power). W. Vogt (*Reine Theorie marktwirtschaftlich-kapitalistischer Systeme. Diskussionsbeiträge zur Politischen Ökonomie*, no. 1, Regensburg 1976) proposes a theory of the market-economy system that combines, in a novel manner, a formal analysis of general equilibrium theory with a critical analysis of the institutional context.

Chapter 2

1. The starting point for the discussion in this chapter has been Marx's treatment of the value-form in *Capital* Volume 1 and elsewhere. In my opinion, however, Marx's presentation is unsatisfactory: it is incomplete, contradictory, and methodologically dubious (especially the principle of the *tertium comparationis*, the reducibility of exchange-values to a 'common substance'). Bailey's perceptive critique of Ricardo's conception of the value-form is also of interest in this context. Marx himself took up a number of Bailey's points, if only to refute them in turn. See Samuel Bailey, *A Critical Dissertation on the Nature, Measure and Cause of Value*, New York 1967; Karl Marx, *Theories of Surplus-Value*, Part III, London 1972. On Marx's presentation and its relation to Bailey, see Ulrich Krause, 'Die Logik der Wertform', *Mehrwert*, 13, Berlin 1977. On Bailey himself, see R.M.

Rauner, *Samuel Bailey and the Classical Theory of Value*, London
1961. The question of the value-form is almost completely ignored in
Marxist literature, and receives banal treatment—well below the level
of Marx himself—in the associated textbooks. One of the few exceptions is I.I. Rubin, *Essays on Marx's Theory of Value*, Detroit 1972.
More recently, a number of interesting but as yet largely unrelated
discussions of the value-form have appeared. See H.G. Backhaus, 'Zur
Dialektik der Wertform', in Alfred Schmidt, ed., *Beiträge zur marxistischen Erkenntnistheorie*, Frankfurt 1969; H.G. Backhaus, 'Mater-
ialien zur Rekonstruktion der Marxschen Werttheorie', 1, 2, 3, in
Gesellschaft, vols. 1, 3, 11, Frankfurt 1974/75/78; J. Nanninga,
*Tauschwert und Wert. Eine sprachkritische Rekonstruktion des
Fundaments der Politischen Ökonomie*, mimeo, Hamburg 1975; D.
von Holt, U. Pasero, V. Roth, *Aspekte der Marxschen Theorie 2. Zur
Wertformenanalyse*, Frankfurt 1974; V. Roth, *Zum wissenschaft-
lichen Ansspruch der Wertformanalyse*, mimeo, Constance 1976; I.
Glaser, *Wertform und Akkumulation*, mimeo, Constance; W. Becker,
Kritik der Marxschen Wertlehre, Hamburg; H. Hagemann, H. Kurz,
G. Magoulas, 'Zum Verhältnis der Marxschen Werttheorie zu den
Wert- und Preis-theorien der Klassiker', *Jahrbücher für National-
ökonomie und Statistik*, vol. 189, 1975, pp. 531-43; K.S. Rehberg, K.G.
Zinn, 'Die Marxsche Wertheorie als Basistheorie interdependenter
Verteilungsstrukturen im Kapitalismus', *Jahrbücher für National-
ökonomie und Statistik*, vol. 191, 1977, pp. 396-427; J. Rancière, 'The
Concept of "Critique" and the "Critique of Political Economy"',
Theoretical Practice, nos. 1, 2, 6; J. Cartelier, *Surproduit et Reproduc-
tion. La Formation de l'économie politique classique*, Grenoble 1976;
J. Schwartz, 'There is Nothing Simple About a Commodity', in J.
Schwartz, ed., *The Subtle Anatomy of Capitalism*, Santa Monica 1977.
The critical studies undertaken by Alfred Sohn-Rethel occupy a
special place in the Marxist analysis of the commodity; although
originally prepared in the 1920s, they were not published until rela-
tively recently. See Alfred Sohn-Rethel, *Warenform und Denkform*,
Frankfurt 1978, which includes Sohn-Rethel's 1936 essay 'Von der
Analytik des Wirtschaftens zur Theorie der Volkswirtschaft'. On
Sohn-Rethel, see H.D. Dombrowski, U. Krause, P. Roos, *Symposium
Warenform-Denkform*, Frankfurt 1978. These works are primarily
critical analyses of Marx's presentation of the value-form itself,
usually aimed at effecting repairs within the framework of Marxist
theory. (With the clear exception of Becker, who is criticized by Hagemann'et al., and Rehberg and Zinn.) As yet there has been no reconstruction of the object of the analysis itself, namely the value-form (cf.
references to the literature in chapters 5 and 6).

    2.   Rancière, 'Critique', *Theoretical Practice*, no. 2 (April 1971),
p. 35.

    3.   Nothing can be asserted about the equivalence of two commod-
ities solely because they stand in a relation to each other; this would

require a third commodity in terms of which each could be 'measured'. If the exchange ratio between C_i and C_j is e_{ij}, this ratio is as good as any other, and permits the deduction neither of equivalence nor of the lack of it. If C_k is a third commodity, then $\frac{e_{ik}}{e_{jk}}$ expresses the exchange ratio between C_i and C_j as 'measured' in C_k. C_i and C_j are equivalent if and only if $\frac{e_{ik}}{e_{jk}} = 1$ (if no other commodity is involved), and this is correspondingly expressed in e_{ij} if and only if $e_{ij} = \frac{e_{ik}}{e_{jk}}$, in other words, if the exchange-structure is consistent. The role played by such structural moments in the shape of a third object can be seen in an example drawn from a completely different domain, the 'hau' of the Maoris. A gives a gift, g, to B; in turn B gives g to C; if C gives a gift h to B, then B has to pass h on as a gift to A (if he doesn't want to tempt fate). The gift h is called the 'hau' of g. 'Ranapiri had merely said that the good given by the third person to the second was the hau of the thing received by the second from the first.' (See Sahlins, *Stone Age Economics*, p. 155). In symbolic terms:

$$A \underset{h}{\overset{g}{\rightleftarrows}} B \underset{h}{\overset{g}{\rightleftarrows}} C.$$

h is a kind of 'return on' or 'product of' of g (Sahlins, p. 157), and this rule of the Maori acquires its meaning only through a third person. If the rule is that 'one man's gift should not be another man's capital, and therefore the fruits of a gift ought to be passed back to the original holder, then the introduction of a third party is necessary.' (Sahlins, p. 160, in which he states his objections to Mauss's spiritual interpretation.)

4. After formulating this view of consistency in critical contrast to Marx's analysis of the value-form, I began to encounter similar approaches from quite a different quarter. In the chapter 'On Exchange', Cournot formulates a relation that is formally equivalent to the consistency requirement; it is based on rates of currency exchange, $c_{i,\,k}$; see Cournot, *Principes*. Walras used Cournot's findings in his observations on market-equilibrium for more than two commodities, a problem recently taken up again by Morishima, who calls the consistency requirement the 'Cournot-Walras condition of no further arbitrage'. See Morishima, *Walras's Economics. A Pure Theory of Capital and Money*, Cambridge 1977, p. 23. The three-commodity case, triangular exchange, also crops up in Wicksell, *Geldzins und Güterpreise* (1898), Aalen 1968, p. 20, and, in an almost identical form to the example given here, in J. Schumpeter, *Das Wesen des Geldes*, Göttingen 1970, p. 19, in connection with the necessity of indirect

exchange and the consequent necessity of money. All these authors regard the consistency requirement as a necessary precondition of equilibrium. Cournot is content to go no further than the reference, 'the transactions of the banks always tend to achieve equality, although it may not be achieved at any given time' (Cournot, p. 25). Wicksell and Schumpeter note that the necessity was first proved by Walras (with the additional comment by Wicksell that Jevons dealt with the problem far from satisfactorily). Morishima, however, comments that Walras's proof was in fact not rigorous, and provides his own. (In fact, Morishima discerns a far more fundamental problem, 'which Walras was also unable to solve'; see Morishima, p. 19.)

There is, nevertheless, a fundamental difference between the view of consistency suggested by these writers, which results from the actions of utility-maximizing individuals, and the perspective elaborated here with the aid of the value-form, in which the relation of individuals to commodities figures explicitly only as a relation between commodities. In my view, Marx's account of the value-form provides a reasonable framework, *cum grano salis*, within which to discuss inconsistency, or in other words, exchange in disequilibrium, since the theory of exchange based on utility-maximizing individuals is now encountering considerable difficulties in both this question and the associated issue of money (in which connection the role of labour in this problematic has not even been articulated, let alone dealt with properly). On this point see the chapter on money and the price-form, along with the bibliographical references. For a fundamental critique of the neoclassical equilibrium theory of exchange, see J. Fradin, *Les fondements logiques de la théorie néoclassique de l'échange*, Grenoble 1976.

5. The study of the interconnection of the production-structure plays a major role in connection with the work of Sraffa, and his distinction between basic and non-basic products. See note 7, chapter 1, and the following chapters, in particular chapter 4. A commodity C_i is a basic product if there is a chain from i to *every j* through production (A); otherwise it is a non-basic product. As yet there has been no corresponding study of the interconnection of the exchange-structure, as undertaken here. In the exchange-structure, a commodity corresponding to Sraffa's basic product would be one that is connected to every other commodity through indirect exchange. Accordingly, the assumption of a connected exchange-structure corresponds to the assumption that all products are basic products, an assumption fundamental to many parts of Sraffa's work.

Chapter 3

1. On the many types of primitive money, see P. Einzig, *Primitive*

Money. J.K. Galbraith provides an entertaining account of modern money in *Money: Whence it Came, Where it Went*, London 1975.
2. Marx, *Capital* Volume 1, chapter 1. For an interpretation of Marx's various drafts on money, see Projektgruppe Entwicklung des Marxschen Systems: Das Kapitel vom Geld, Berlin 1973. On Marxist theories of money, see also the literature cited in note 1 of chapter 2, especially H.G. Backhaus, and Suzanne de Brunhoff, *Marx on Money*, New York 1976; H. Visser, 'Marx on Money', *Kredit und Kapital*, vol. 10, pp. 266-87. Unfortunately, the discussion of money in Marxist literature is largely sterile; in only a few instances is any real analysis of the value-form developed. In recent years a debate has arisen about the questionable role of money in general equilibrium theory. See F.H. Hahn, 'On Some Problems of Proving the Existence of an Equilibrium in a Monetary Economy', in F.H. Hahn, F. Brechling, eds., *The Theory of Interest Rates*, London 1965; R.W. Clower, 'A Reconsideration of the Microfoundations of Monetary Theory', in *Western Economic Journal*, vol. 6, 1967, pp. 1-9 (both papers also appear in R.W. Clower, ed., *Monetary Theory: Selected Readings*, Harmondsworth 1969, together with other relevant material). See too, J.M. Ostroy, R.M. Starr, 'Money and the Decentralization of Exchange', in *Econometrica*, vol. 42, 1974, pp. 1093-1113; R. Pethig, *Zur Theorie der Transaktionen. Ein Beitrag zur mikroökonomischen Grundlegung der Geldtheorie*, Tübingen 1975; F.H. Hahn, 'On Non-Walrasian Equilibria', *Review of Economic Studies*, vol. 45, 1978, pp. 1-16. On the various approaches, see F. Haslinger, *Zur mikroökonomischen Fundierung der Geldtheorie*, 1978, which also cites additional relevant material. An overview can also be found in E.R. Weintraub, 'The Microfoundations of Macroeconomics: a Critical Survey', in *Journal of Economic Literature*, vol. 15, 1977, pp. 1-21; see too the papers included in G. Harcourt, ed., *The Microeconomic Foundations of Macroeconomics*, London 1977, and the issue on 'Equilibre général et monnai' in the journal *Economie Appliquée*, volume 30, no. 4, 1977. A survey from the standpoint of the costs of exchange is A.M. Ulph, D.T. Ulph, 'Transaction Costs in General Equilibrium Theory—A Survey', *Economica*, vol. 42, 1975, pp. 355-371. A model that adequately depicts the role of money 'must distinguish between abstract exchange opportunities at some notionally called prices and actual transaction opportunities' (Hahn, 'On Some Problems') and 'the central difficulty in studying non-Walrasian economies... is the distinction between the trading possibilities as perceived by an agent and the "true" trading possibilities' (Hahn, 'On Non-Walrasian Equilibria', p. 1). The problem can be traced back to Walras's treatment of multi-commodity exchange; although he acknowledged the existence of a problem of consistency in exchange involving more than two commodities, he did not distinguish between 'a planned exchange of x for z from a planned pair of exchanges—one of x for y and one of y for z'; see P.W. Howitt,

'Walras and Monetary Theory', *Western Economic Journal*, vol. 11, 1973, p. 493, which gives a very clear presentation of this problem. See also Morishima's book on Walras, already cited. A further point in this debate is the question of how the role of money in Keynes's theory should be interpreted: see P. Davidson, *Money and the Real World*, 2nd edn, London 1978, and O. Steiger, 'Prelude to a Theory of a Monetary Economy. A Note on the Origins of Modern Macroeconomics', in *Diskussionsbeiträge zur Politischen Ökonomie*, no. 3, Bremen 1978. As early as 1933 Keynes himself criticized the customary concept of a 'Real Exchange Economy... which uses money but uses it merely as a neutral link between transactions in real things', and in its place suggested a 'monetary theory of production'. See J.M. Keynes, 'A Monetary Theory of Production', in *Der Stand und die nächste Zukunft der Konjunkturforschung. Festschrift für A. Spiethoff*, Berlin 1933, pp. 123-125.

3.   This corresponds to Clower's definition of a money-commodity; see R.W. Clower, 'A Reconsideration...', p. 206. The linking of the definition of money to the special relation of direct exchange τ, however, affords a very narrow concept of money, as will be shown later. Such a money-commodity seldom exists. The notion here seems to be that money is necessary if not all acts of exchange are direct—in other words, when the direct-exchange relation is incomplete and thus requires indirect mediation through a money-commodity. A further necessity for money arises if there are 'too few' such acts of exchange, such that indirect exchange is also incomplete. This is possible even in a connected direct-exchange structure, without the existence of a money-commodity in Clower's sense. This will be illustrated below.

4.   Usually the concept of a barter economy will be meant for the particular direct-exchange relation τ; see Clower, 'A Reconsideration', p. 206. However, Clower treats the 'transitivity of the exchange relation' and the proposition that 'any commodity... can be traded directly for all other commodities' as synonymous with barter, which mars his subsequent discussion of a money-commodity. These aspects are differentiated here as barter and quasi-barter economies. (Clower's arguments touch on the points raised here in connection with the value-form; his discussion of the direct-exchange relation, however, contains no mention of *quantities* of commodities.)

5.   On the concept of a pure money economy, see Clower, 'A Reconsideration', p. 207.

6.   Cf. Clower, Hahn, and other criticisms of the concept of money in general (neo-Walrasian) equilibrium theory. Walras himself writes in connection with multi-commodity exchange: 'full or general equilibrium of the market exists only if the relative price of any two commodities is equal to the ratio of the prices of either of them to any desired third'. (L. Walras, *Mathematische Theorie der Preisbestimmung der wirtschaftlichen Güter. Vier Denkschriften*. Glashütten

1972, p. 29.) This corresponds to the assertion here that for any three commodities $e_{ij} = \dfrac{e_{ik}}{e_{jk}}$ (in Walras's terminology $p_{c,\,b} = \dfrac{p_{c,\,a}}{p_{b,\,a}}$ for three commodities A, B, C.) In other words: a Walrasian equilibrium exists if and only if all commodities are money-commodities that induce the same money relation, which means: if and only if a uniform money-commodity exists, or to put it another way, if and only if the economy under consideration is a barter economy. After showing that such an equilibrium is *theoretically* possible, Walras continues: 'It thus remains to demonstrate, and this is the main point, that the problem of exchange which we have just solved in theory is the same one solved in practice on the market through the mechanism of free competition.' (Ibid., p. 33). The criticism mentioned is relevant precisely to this 'main point'; see also P.W. Howitt.

7. The question of the circulation of commodities and money is not taken up by Sraffa, or in works related to Sraffa. Nevertheless, prices, especially the positivity of prices, play a central role. In view of the example of the three basic products between which there is no direct act of change, it would be reasonable to ask how these prices come about, or indeed what they might mean. (Morishima discusses one case similar to the examples above; see Morishima, *Walras' Economics*, p. 204. One possible way of avoiding 'this kind of perversity is to prohibit individuals and firms from demanding a commodity unless they have enough money'. Ibid., p. 204.) This question may arise in connection with the emergence of negative prices in certain types of production-structures. (On negative prices, see Sraffa's example of 'beans', *Production of Commodities*, p. 90, and the literature referred to in note 7, chapter 1.) Remak has suggested that Sraffa's prices could be denoted 'imputed prices' (*supponierte Preise*). As early as 1929 Remak had studied the problem of exchange (independently of production) and offered a solution formally equivalent to Sraffa's price system for the case in which there is no surplus product. (R. Remak, 'Kann die Volkswirtschaftslehre eine exakte Wissenschaft werden?', in *Jahrbücher für Nationalökonomie und Statistik*, vol. 131, 1929, pp. 703-735. P. Newman refers to Remak's similarities to Sraffa in P. Newman, 'Production of Commodities by Means of Commodities', in *Schweizerische Zeitschrift für Volkswirtschaft und Statistik*, vol. 98, 1962, pp. 58-75. Remak's paper discusses the dependence of the positivity of prices on the interconnected structure of the matrix (without the now-customary Perron-Frobenius theorems). For a detailed study of Remak's exchange problem, see D. Gale, *The Theory of Linear Economic Models*, New York 1960. For Remak's biography, see W. Wittmann, 'Die extremale Wirtschaft. Robert Remak—ein Vorläufer der Aktivitätsanalyse', in *Jahrbücher für Nationalökonomie und Statistik*, vol. 180, 1967, pp. 397-409. In the terminology employed here (see chapter 2), Remak's Problem runs as follows. For given

quantities $y_{ij} \geq 0$, prices $p_i (i, j, = 1, 2, \ldots, n)$ are sought such that for every commodity-owner expenditure will equal income. Thus:

$$\sum_{i=1}^{n} y_{ij} p_i = p_j \cdot \sum_{k=1}^{n} y_{jk} \quad \text{for every } j$$

There is always a solution to the problem with non-negative prices, but some (though not all) prices could be zero. In view of zero-prices, one could, more generally, seek positive exchange ratios z_{ij} that solve the system

$$\sum_{i=1}^{n} y_{ij} z_{ij} = \sum_{k=1}^{n} y_{jk} \quad \text{for every } j$$

Consistent solutions of this system (i.e. the matrix Z of the z_{ij} is consistent) would thus correspond to solutions through a system of positive imputed prices. That a solution with positive prices is not always possible means that a consistent circulation among commodity-owners is not always possible.

8. According to Aristotle, money (*nomisma*) 'is so called because it exists not by nature but by custom' (*nomos*). (Aristotle, *The Nichomachean Ethics*, trans. J.A.K. Thompson, revised edn, Harmondsworth 1976, p. 184.) To this day, political economy is less clear about the meaning of custom than it is about the fact that it does not owe its existence to nature.

9. Clower, 'A Reconsideration', pp. 207-8. This 'restriction' was already a 'central theme' of Marx, who provided a clear and detailed study of this point through the pattern $C-M-C$. See *Capital* Volume 1, p. 188 ff. and de Brunhoff, *Marx on Money*. It is interesting that it is here that Marx discusses the possibility (though not yet the reality) of crisis. There is a certain parallel in contemporary discussion of money, in the emphasis on such phenomena as 'insolvency' and 'bankruptcy'. (See Hahn, in Clower, *Monetary Theory*, p. 200-1.) Of course, Marx's model is highly abstract and thus does not encompass the structural specifics of money presented here in the deduced propositions and illustrative examples.

10. That the 'value' of money depends on its quantity is a very old idea. For one of the first systematic, albeit vaguely formulated, discussions of it see D. Hume, 'Of Money', in A.A. Walters, ed., *Money and Banking*, Harmondsworth 1973. Wicksell's *Geldzins* also provides a classic formulation of the question, as does Irving Fisher, *The Purchasing Power of Money*, New York 1911. Fisher's own careful treatment of the equation of exchange is superior to current, often superficial, textbook presentations. On more recent monetarist formulations, see M. Friedman, *The Optimum Quantity of Money and Other Essays*, Chicago 1969, in particular his 1956 essay 'The Quantity Theory of Money—A Restatement'; K. Brunner, 'Eine Neuformulierung der

Quantitätstheorie des Geldes', *Kredit und Kapital*, vol. 3, 1970, pp. 1-29. (Fisher had in fact already intended to undertake a 'reconstruction' of the quantity theory). One fundamental difference between Fisher's 'algebraic presentation of the equation of exchange' and many associated presentations on the one hand and the approach adopted here on the other is this (in our notation). Fisher considered the 'total amount expended', N, from two sides. On the one hand, $N =$

$$\sum_{i=1}^{n} N_i, \text{ where } N_i = \sum_{j=1}^{n} x_{ij} = \sum_{j=1}^{n} y_{ji} p_j \text{ is the amount expended by}$$

the i-th person. On the other, he divides this total amount *expended* according to the 'net velocity of circulation' of notes and coin, $N =$

$$\sum_{s=1}^{n(n-1)} m_s \cdot s = S \text{ (*), and defines } v = \frac{N}{M} \text{ where } M = \sum_{s=1}^{n(n-1)} m_s. \text{ It is}$$

clear that the equation of exchange $y \cdot p = N = v \cdot M$ then holds. The identification in (*) of the expenditure (N) and the transaction-sum (S) is not made. Fisher was forced to regard them as identical, since he considered neither the structure of transactions nor the localization of the sum of money. Only by considering both these structural aspects is it possible to counterpose intended expenditure (N) to the expenditure (S) that can actually occur through a particular sum of money under a given transaction structure. Nevertheless, it remains the case that 'it is much easier to criticize the quantity theory than to replace it with a better and more correct theory.' (Wicksell, *Geldzins*, p. 39.)

11.   This classical contention has been much criticized and frequently improved upon. However, it seems to me well suited to the task of demonstrating some of the conceptual differences within the quantity theory. See also P. Samuelson, 'What Classical and Neo-Classical Monetary Theory Really Was', *Canadian Journal of Economics*, vol. 1, 1968, pp. 1-15. The intention here is to show that even in a simple model, where money is considered solely as a means of circulation, the transaction-structure and localization are relevant in determining the connection between prices and the sum of money.

Chapter 4

1.   Such unproductivity could be relevant when analysing not the production of use-values but the elimination of non-use values, such as waste, toxic materials, and so on. See also the note on joint-production in chapter 1.
2.   A number of formulations have been suggested for the calculation of the quantities of direct and indirect labour expended to produce

a commodity—although most apply only to the special case in which labour is treated as homogeneous (cf. Sraffa, *Production of Commodities*, p. 89; Morishima, *Marx's Economics*, p. 10 ff; Pasinetti, *Lectures*, p. 76, who denotes these expenditures of homogeneous direct labour as 'vertically integrated labour coefficients'). The most common method is the determination of so-called labour-values. The labour-value λ_i of a unit of a commodity, which measures the social expenditure of homogeneous labour, is obtained through the system of equations

$$\sum_{j=1}^{n} a_{ji}\lambda_j + l_i = \lambda_i \qquad (i = 1, 2, \ldots, n).$$

For a formal translation of this approach to a system with heterogeneous labour, see S. Bowles, H. Gintis, 'The Marxian Theory of Value and Heterogeneous Labour: a Critique and Reformulation', *Cambridge Journal of Economics*, vol. 1, 1977, p. 186. However, this 'metaphysical method of determining socially necessary labour-time' (C.C. von Weizsäcker, 'Notizen zur Marxschen Wertlehre', in Nutzinger/Wolfstetter, *Die Marxsche Theorie*, II, p. 98) is quite unsatisfactory. First, the starting point is the existence of individual commodity-values, for which the equation system effectively postulates a sort of 'axiom of the retention of labour-time in the production process' (Weizsäcker, ibid., p. 99). Second, this method encounters serious difficulties when faced with joint-production. In view of these difficulties, made clear in 'Steedman's Paradox', a number of other suggestions have been made for the concept of a 'labour-value', in particular Morishima's notion of 'true values'. See M. Morishima, C. Catephores, *Value, Exploitation and Growth. Marx in the Light of Modern Economic Theory*, London 1978; E. Wolfstetter, *Wert, Profitrate und Beschäftigung. Aspekte der Marxschen und der klassischen Wirtschaftstheorie*, Frankfurt 1977; I. Steedman, *Marx after Sraffa*, London 1977. For a further conceptualization, and a critique of previous notions of 'labour-value', see D. Hinrichsen, U. Krause, *Choice of Technique*, mimeo, Bremen 1978. Although the method employed in the coal-iron example, and for Proposition 1, leads formally to the same result as the application of the 'metaphysical method' to heterogeneous labour, it nevertheless quite clearly exposes (since no 'labour-values' are postulated) the assumptions under which it is proper to speak of the expenditures of labour for an individual unit of a commodity. The 'metaphysical method' can also be formally applied to systems with joint-production, but as Steedman has shown, this procedure does not yield meaningful results. The method employed for Proposition 1 also yields non-negative expenditures of labour in joint-production systems for any non-negative net product y *producible* under that system—but since a net product in a joint-production system generally does not consist of an individual commodity, it is not meaningful to attribute any expenditure of labour to a commodity that cannot be produced on its own. And since the 'metaphysical method' assumes *individual* commodity-values from the outset, this method will necessarily lead to disparities when applied to joint-production.

3. Proposition 1 can be extended to the general case by the same method: instead of one type of labour, *m* types of labour are directly required to produce a commodity. Instead of the diagonal matrix *L*, we then have an $m \times n$ matrix *L*, whose elements l_{ij} indicate the direct expenditure of labour of type *i* required to produce C_j. The expression will then read

$$(\bar{l}_{1j} \text{ type } 1, \ldots, \bar{l}_{mj} \text{ type } m) \to C_j \qquad (j = 1, \ldots, n)$$

where $\bar{l}_{ij} = \sum_{k=1}^{n} l_{ik} \, v_{kj}$. (Cf. U. Krause, 'Elemente einer multisektoralen Analyse'.)

Chapter 5

1. Marx, *Capital* Volume 1, pp. 166-7. Marx accompanies this idea, essentially correct in my view, with other notions such as the deduction of abstract labour through the principle of a common third element, a physiological interpretation of abstract labour (sheer expenditure of brain and muscle), and abstract labour as a mental abstraction. These conceptions, popular among Marxists and anti-Marxists alike, seem untenable to me, for various reasons. Interesting expositions of abstract labour, a central idea of Marx's work, include I.I. Rubin, *Essays on Marx's Theory of Value*, chapter 14; Lucio Colletti, *From Rousseau to Lenin*, London 1972; Geoffrey Kay, 'A Note on Abstract Labour', *Bulletin of the Conference of Socialist Economists*, March 1976; C.J. Arthur, 'The Concept of Abstract Labour', *Bulletin of the Conference of Socialist Economists*, October 1976. (In general, the more philosophically oriented writers are more productive than the economists.) See also the literature cited in note 1, chapter 2. For a discussion of various expositions of abstract labour and of Marx's informative critique of Bailey in this connection (emphasizing the 'space of labour'), see U. Krause, *Logik*.

2. The relation $\dfrac{p_i}{p_j} = \dfrac{\lambda_i}{\lambda_j}$ is customarily discussed under the assumption of *homogeneous* labour, under the catch-phrase 'proportionality of values and prices'. The usual assessment of this relation is then that it does indeed apply to simple commodity production, but not to capitalist commodity production. For an alternative appraisal, see R. Picard, 'Zum quantitativen Wertproblem', in *Gesellschaft*, H.G. Backhaus *et al.*, ed., vol. 3, Frankfurt 1975. If homogeneous labour is

assumed, it is difficult to see why there should be *any* connection between the entirely disparate systems of price and value. To my knowledge, no one has ever proven the asserted proportionality for simple commodity production. This point will be taken up again in chapter 6. Here, in contrast, the fundamental relation (with quantitatively undetermined labour-values!) emerges simultaneous with the derivation of the concept of abstract labour. The intent of the fundamental relation is not to 'explain' relative prices by relative labour-values, but simply to establish the particular relation between production and circulation in a market economy. And as usual, an equation does not in itself entail any causal direction. Doubts about the fundamental relation thus cannot rest merely on the distinction between simple and capitalist commodity production, but must focus on the assumptions made in the construction of abstract labour, in particular the monotonicity of Θ—which would then raise the question of how to portray abstract labour properly.

3.   P. Sraffa, *Production of Commodities*, pp. 90 ff. See also the literature cited in note 7, chapter 1.

4.   A. Smith, *The Wealth of Nations*, Harmondsworth 1970, pp. 150-1.

Chapter 6

1.   D. Ricardo, *The Principles of Political Economy and Taxation*, London 1973, p. 7; A. Smith, *The Wealth of Nations*, p. 150. Despite its simplicity (no capital stock, no consideration of land), this example is interesting, and has been the subject of repeated discussion. Cf. F.H. Knight, 'Die Grenznutzenlehre', in A. Montaner, ed., *Geschichte der Volkswirtschaftslehre*, Cologne 1967; Joan Robinson, *Economic Philosophy*, Harmondsworth 1962; T.D. Willett, 'A Defence of A. Smith's Deer and Beaver Model', *The Journal of Economic Studies*, vol. 3/2, 1968, pp. 29-32; Maurice Dobb, *Theories of Value and Distribution Since Adam Smith. Ideology and Economic Theory*, London 1973.

2.   The literature on the labour theory of value and its unloved child, the transformation problem, is now boundless. References to some relevant literature have already been given in chapter 1, note 7 (points 1 and 2), and chapter 2, note 1. See as well the contributions by Nuti, Shaikh, Medio, Colletti, and Schwartz in the collection, J. Schwartz, ed., *The Subtle Anatomy of Capitalism*, Santa Monica 1977, and those by Glombowski, Buhbe, Krüger, Flaschel, Krause, and Teplitz in *Mehrwert 13: Beiträge zum Transformationsproblem*, Berlin 1977. References to relevant works are also provided in *Mehrwert 13*. Dobb's book provides ideological background to the history of the debate. On questions of methodology, see A. Sen, 'On the Labour

Theory of Value: Some Methodological Issues', *Cambridge Journal of Economics*, vol. 2, 1978, pp. 175-190, and the appended bibliography.

3. Cf. chapter 4, note 2, and the references given there to Morishima, Steedman, and Wolfstetter.

4. It is worth noting that, with the exception of Marx, through whose work the question of differing forms of coordination runs like a *leitmotiv*, the political economists undertook scarcely any precise investigation of the various early forms of social coordination of the division of labour. Instead the question of coordination was exemplified by a solitary man, Robinson Crusoe, living on an isolated island—in other words, a direct and conscious form of coordination (assuming Robinson was not schizophrenic), poles apart from the indirect price coordination of a market economy. Only recently, in the compass of an 'economic anthropology', have various earlier forms of coordination been the subject of close investigation. See for example, Sahlins, *Stone Age Economics*.

5. Cf. Krause, *Elemente*, in which this dogma is discussed especially in connection with theories associated with Sraffa and Marx. For a critique of the deer-beaver example under heterogeneous labour, see F.H. Knight, 'Die Grenznutzenlehre'.

6. On this question, see H. Gintis, 'The Nature of Labor Exchange and the Theory of Capitalist Production', *Review of Radical Political Economy*, vol. 8, 1976, pp. 36-54. The wage rates paid for individual concrete labours will be examined more closely in chapter 7.

7. A predetermined structure of real wages (or often simply: the real wage) is assumed not only by Marxist authors, but also by those of Sraffian persuasion. Steedman's attack on Marx's theory of value derives much of its force precisely from the fact that the structure of real wages B is assumed to be given. As is easily seen, if $w_i = w_i'$ it follows that $p = (1 + r) \cdot p(A + BL)$, where p are prices of production, r the uniform rate of profit, BL wages advanced (see chapter 7). On this basis, through the Perron-Frobenius root of the irreducible matrix $A + BL$, an unambiguous determination of relative prices of production *and* the rate of profit is obtained—without any mention of values. (See Steedman, *Marx after Sraffa*, pp. 50 ff.). Although formally unobjectionable, this method is economically unsatisfactory, since it treats the real wage as an independent instead of a dependent (on money) variable. To paraphrase Bertrand Russell, the advantage of this method is reminiscent of theft: you just take what you need.

8. Case 1 corresponds to Sraffa's theory, in which no reproduction-point is singled out, so that the reproduction curve becomes a wage-profit curve (in which wages are not part of costs, as they are here). Case 2 basically corresponds to the situation considered by Marx. Of course, Marx does make statements about wages that do not correspond to a $q = 1$ situation; see K. Gerlach, 'Zur Marxschen Lohntheorie', *Jahrbuch für Sozialwissenschaft*, vol. 24, 1973, pp. 145-59.

Situations corresponding to case 3 are examined by G. Maarek, *Introduction au 'Capital' de Karl Marx*, p. 151, and by G. Abraham-Frois and E. Berrebi, *Théorie de la Valeur*, p. 257. Case 4 seems uninteresting. But it does have some meaning in comparing several reproduction curves. An example may illustrate the point. Let *A* be a highly-industrialized and *B* an underdeveloped country, so that the reproduction curve of *A* is always well above that of *B*. Now, if the rate of profit is the same in both countries, the reproduction index will generally lie above the reproduction-point in *A* and below it in *B*. In *A* workers participate in the higher rate of surplus-value of the country, whereas capital in *B* has to compete with capital of country *A* (uniform rate of profit), so the workers in *B* are paid less than their reproduction price.

9. Cf. the Morishima-Okishio theorem on the connection between the rate of surplus-value and the rate of profit, generalized by Morishima (through 'true values') to the case of joint-production. This has since become a topic of lively debate as 'the fundamental Marxian theorem'. See M. Morishima and G. Catephores, *Value, Exploitation and Growth* for the most recent presentation of this theorem and its history. This theorem is more complex than the discussion here, since its point is to establish a connection between a positive rate of surplus-value and a positive rate of profit without any direct connection between values and prices (like the fundamental relation here). The fundamental theorem, of course, deals with neither the reproduction index nor the case of 'unhealthy' surplus-value. On the central role of the assumption of a subsistence wage in the fundamental theorem, see H.G. Nutzinger, 'Concepts of Value in Linear Economic Models', *Operations Research Verfahren*, 26, 1977, pp. 717-24. For an analysis of the rate of surplus-value in connection with Sraffa's standard commodity, see J. Eatwell, 'Mr Sraffa's Standard Commodity and the Rate of Exploitation', *Quarterly Journal of Economics*, vol. 89, 1975, pp. 534-55.

Chapter 7

1. The measure α_{ij} in which one hour of labour of type i is equated with an hour of labour of type j as abstract labour may depend on such diverse factors as the sex, age, race, or even religious affiliation of the workers (it varies from country to country). The influence of these factors has been analysed at the level of empirically accessible wage rates in studies on segmented labour-markets. See R.C. Edwards, D. Gordon, N. Reich, *Labor Market Segmentation*, Lexington 1975, and for a critical survey, G.G. Cain, 'The Challenge of Segmented Labor Market Theories to Orthodox Theory: A Survey', *Journal of Economic Literature*, 1977, pp. 1215-57. A theoretical approach to this question

can be found in S. Bowles, H. Gintis, 'The Marxian Theory of Value and Heterogeneous Labour', *Cambridge Journal of Economics*, 1, 1977. See also U. Krause, 'Elemente'. The significance of studies of segmented labour-markets for analysis of abstract labour is that they demolish the dogma of homogeneous labour.

2. For references to Sraffa's standard commodity, the system of prices of production with homogeneous labour, and the wage-profit relation, see chapter 1, note 7.

3. The assumptions of a uniform rate of profit and a uniform wage-rate relate to quite distinct equalization processes (the rate of profit is a rate, the wage-rate is a price). One assumption thus does not imply the other. Sraffa explicitly assumes uniformity of both rate of profit and wages (see *Production of Commodities*, paragraphs 4 and 10); the same applies, virtually without exception, to the Sraffa-oriented literature. It is possible, however, to investigate both varying sectoral rates of profit and varying wage-rates within this framework. On the connection between the structure of profit-rates and monopolization, see U. Krause, 'Die allgemeine Struktur des Monopols', *Probleme des Klassemkampfs*, Heft 24, 1976, pp. 87-130. On the case of several primary factors in the shape of labour and land, which in formal terms resembles that of several types of labour, see J.S. Metcalfe, I. Steedman, 'Reswitching and Primary Input Use', *Economic Journal*, vol. 82, 1972, pp. 140-157, and the continuation of these arguments in G. Abraham-Frois, E. Berrebi, 'Théorie', and I. Steedman, *Marx after Sraffa*. For a detailed analysis of land of differential quality, see H.D. Kurz, 'Zur neoricardianischen Theorie', and H.D. Kurz, 'Rent Theory in a Multi-sectoral Model', *Oxford Economic Papers*, vol. 30, 1978, pp. 16-37. For a treatment of differential wage-rates whilst assuming that $w = pB$, see S. Bowles, H. Gintis, 'The Marxian Theory', and the associated argumentation in I. Steedman, *Marx after Sraffa*.

4. For Sraffa's quote, see *Production of Commodities*, p. 18. For a detailed analysis of the scarcely broached question of an invariant measure of value in classical political economy and its relation to the standard commodity and the wage-profit relation, see H.D. Kurz, 'Zur neoricardianischen Theorie'; L. Pasinetti, *Lectures on the Theory of Production*; A. Roncaglia, *Sraffa and the Theory of Prices*. Consideration of Sraffa's standard commodity from the standpoint of abstract labour is not usual, but it does shed new light on Sraffa's construction. For the case of *homogeneous* labour, Pasinetti refers to the duality between Sraffa's standard commodity and a particular proportioning of direct expenditures of labour, l. This special case for the relation between A and l—namely $lA = \varrho l$—corresponds to the special case of a uniform organic composition. See Pasinetti, *Lectures*, and in particular, the footnotes on pp. 79, 100, and 119. In contrast, in the framework of *abstract labour* there is a standard reduction for every l (where A is

connected). Consequently, the standard reduction does not correspond to a uniform organic composition in the conventional sense.

5. The traditional concept of organic composition is narrow in two ways: it is based on the dogma of homogeneous labour, and it treats labour-power like any other, produced commodity. Correspondingly, this restricted notion of organic composition is uniform only in a special and trivial production-structure. As we have already noted, in the system (S) the *assumption that* $w = pB$ implies that $\lambda A = k^2 \lambda BL$ is equivalent to the standard reduction. On the *assumption of homogeneous* labour, it then follows that $\lambda A = k^2 \lambda BL$ is equivalent to $lA = \varrho l$, and thus equivalent to a very special production-structure, indeed trivial in the present context. In the framework of the system (S) the assumption that $w = pB$ corresponds to the assumption that the relative price of the commodity labour-power, which means the relative wage-rate, is equal to the relative *re*production value of labour-power —an arbitrary extension of the fundamental relation to the commodity labour-power, in which the reproduction-value serves as the 'value of the commodity labour-power' just as if it were a manufactured commodity. The reason why uniformity of the organic composition collapses into the simple case of $lA = \varrho l$ thus lies in the dogma of homogeneous labour combined with the treatment of labour-power as a produced commodity. Cf. the remarks on reproduction in chapter 6, section 2, and the discussion of the transformation problem in the present chapter.

6. In the present context, the problem of reduction, like reduction-coefficients, always relates to the 'equating' (Θ) of varying concrete labours as distinct quantities of abstract labour. This should not be confused with another question, also called a reduction problem, namely that of the reduction of 'complex' to 'simple' labour—a rather dubious procedure. On 'complexity' as a characteristic of abstract labour, see D. Hinrichsen, 'Zum Problem der Reduktion komplizierter auf einfache Arbeit', in E. Altvater, F. Huisken, eds., *Materialien zur politischen Ökonomie des Ausbildungssektors*, Erlangen 1971; see also U. Krause, 'Elemente' and its accompanying bibliography. For a quite different treatment of the transformation problem, see the chapter entitled 'The Transformation Problem: A Markov Process', in M. Morishima and G. Catephores, *Value, Exploitation and Growth*; and A. Shaikh, 'Marx's Theory of Value and the "Transformation Problem"', in J. Schwartz, ed., *The Subtle Anatomy of Capitalism*. (N. Okishio had already published a similar approach in Japanese in 1972; cf. Morishima and Catephores, *Value, Exploitation and Growth*, p. 166). This treatment goes beyond the proportionality of values and prices and suggests an iterative solution of the transformation of 'prices into prices', beginning with Marx's transformation of values into prices as a first step.

7. Some of these tests can be found in U. Krause, 'Elemente', and

Krause, *Über negative Werte*, mimeo, Bremen 1977. There it is shown that a model of a non-diagonal L can be used to depict the economically important question of the relation between the division of labour in the factory and the division of labour in society. It is further shown that a standard reduction does not always exist when L is non-diagonal. A non-connected A was discussed earlier in the beans and deer-beaver examples (see chapter 7, section 2) where it emerged that there was either no standard reduction or an endless number of them. As for joint-production, although it can be shown on the one hand that the exchange curve is negative for some values of the reduction-coefficients (in particular those corresponding to homogeneous labour), on the other hand there exists a standard reduction corresponding to positive exchange ratios and positive commodity values. This sheds new light on the problem of negative values, a frequent topic of discussion recently in connection with Steedman's paradox. See also Morishima and Catephores, *Value, Exploitation and Growth*; I. Steedman, *Marx after Sraffa*; E. Wolfstetter, *Wert, Profitrate und Beschäftigung*.

Bibliography

Abraham-Frois, G. and Berrebi, E., *Théorie de la Valeur, des Prix et de l'Accumulation*, Paris 1976.

Arthur, C.J., 'The Concept of Abstract Labour', *Bulletin of the Conference of Socialist Economists*, October 1976.

Backhaus, H.G., 'Zur Dialektik der Wertform', *Beiträge zur marxistischen Erkenntnistheorie*, Frankfurt 1969.

——, 'Materialien zur Rekonstruktion der Marxschen Werttheorie 1, 2, 3', *Gesellschaft*, Bd. 1, 3, 11. Frankfurt 1974/75/78.

Bailey, S., *A Critical Dissertation on the Nature, Measure and Cause of Value*, New York 1967 (originally published 1825).

Becker, W., *Kritik der Marxschen Wertlehre*, Hamburg 1972.

Bowles, S. and Gintis, H., 'The Marxian Theory of Value and Heterogeneous Labour: a Critique and Reformulation', *Cambridge Journal of Economics*, vol. 1, 1977, pp. 173-192.

Bródy, A., *Proportions, Prices and Planning. A Mathematical Restatement of the Labour Theory of Value*, Amsterdam 1970.

Brüggemann, E. and Werner, A., 'Theorie der Zerlegbarkeit nichtnegativer Matrizen und ihre Anwendung in der mathematischen Ökonomie', mimeo, Bremen 1978.

de Brunhoff, S., *Marx On Money*, New York 1976.

Brunner, K., 'Eine Neuformulierung der Quantitätstheorie des Geldes', *Kredit und Kapital*, Bd. 3, 1970, pp. 1-29.

Cain, G.G., 'The Challenge of Segmented Labor Market Theories to Orthodox Theory: A Survey', *Journal of Economic Literature*, 1977, pp. 1215-57.

Cartelier, J., *Surproduit et Reproduction. La formation de l'économie politique classique*, Grenoble 1976.

Clower, R.W., 'A Reconsideration of the Microfoundations of Monetary Theory', *Western Economic Journal*, vol. 6, 1967, pp. 1-9.

——, ed., *Monetary Theory. Selected Readings*, Harmondsworth 1969.

——, 'What Traditional Monetary Theory Really Wasn't', *Canadian Journal of Economics*, vol. 2, 1969, pp. 299-302.

Cogoy, M., *Wertstruktur und Preisstruktur. Die Bedeutung der linearen Produktionstheorie für die Kritik der politischen Ökonomie*, Frankfurt 1977.

Colletti, L., *From Rousseau to Lenin*, London 1972.

Commons, J.R., 'Legal Foundations of Capitalism', Madison 1968 (first published 1924).

Cournot, A., *Untersuchungen über die mathematischen Grundlagen der Theorie des Reichtums*, Jena 1924 (first published 1863).

Davidson, P., *Money and the Real World*, 2nd edn., London 1978.

Dobb, M., *Theories of Value and Distribution Since Adam Smith. Ideology and Economic Theory*, London 1973.

Dorfman, R., Samuelson, P.A., and Solow, R.M., *Linear Programming and Economic Analysis*, New York 1958.

Dombrowski, H.D., Krause, U., and Roos, P., *Symposium Warenform-Denkform*, Frankfurt 1978.

Eatwell, J., 'Mr. Sraffa's Standard Commodity and the Rate of Exploitation', *Quarterly Journal of Economics*, vol. 89, 1975, pp. 543-555.

Edwards, R.C., Gordon, D., and Reich, N., *Labour Market Segmentation*, Lexington 1975.

Einzig, P., *Primitive Money. In Its Ethnological, Historical and Economic Aspects*, 2nd edn, Oxford 1966.

Fisher, I., *Die Kaufkraft des Geldes*, Berlin 1916.

Fradin, J., *Les Fondements logiques de la théorie néoclassique de l'échange*, Grenoble 1976.

Gale, D., *The Theory of Linear Economic Models*, New York 1960.

Gantmacher, F.R., *Matrizenrechnung*, 2 Bände, Berlin 1970.

Georgescu-Roegen, N., *The Entropy Law and the Economic Process*, Cambridge Mass. 1971.

Gerlach, K., 'Zur Marxschen Lohntheorie', *Jahrbuch für Sozialwissenschaft*, Bd. 24, 1973, pp. 145-159.

Gilbert, J.C., 'The Demand for Money: the Development of an Economic Concept', *Journal of Political Economy*, vol. 61, 1953, pp. 144-59.

Gintis, H., 'The Nature of Labor Exchange and the Theory of Capitalist Production', *Review of Radical Political Economics*, vol. 8, 1976, pp. 36-54.

Glaser, I., 'Wertform und Akkumulation', mimeo, Konstanz, n.d.

Godelier, M., *Rationality and Irrationality in Economics*, London 1972.

Hagemann, H., Kurz, H., and Magoulas, G., 'Zum Verhältnis der Marxschen Werttheorie zu den Wert- und Preistheorien der Klassiker', *Jahrbücher für Nationalökonomie und Statistik*, Bd. 189, 1975, pp. 531-43.

Hahn, F.H., 'On Some Problems of Proving the Existence of an Equilibrium in a Monetary Economy', in F.H. Hahn, F. Brechling, eds., *The Theory of Interest Rates*, London 1965.

——, 'On Non-Walrasian Equilibria', *Review of Economic Studies*, vol. 45, 1978, pp. 1-16.

Harcourt, G.C., ed., *The Microeconomic Foundations of Macroeconomics*, London 1977.

Haslinger, F., *Zur mikroökonomischen Fundierung der Geldtheorie*, 1978.

Hildenbrand, K., and Hildenbrand, W., *Lineare ökonomische Modelle*, Berlin 1975.

Hinrichsen, D., 'Zum Problem der Reduktion komplizierter auf einfache Arbeit', in E. Altvater, F. Huisken, eds., *Materialien zur politischen Ökonomie des Ausbildungssektors*, Erlangen 1971.

Hinrichsen, D., Krause, U., 'Choice of Technique in Joint Production Models', in *Operations Research Verfahren*.

Hirshleifer, J., 'Exchange Theory: the Missing Chapter', *Western Economic Journal*, vol. 11, 1973, pp. 129-46.

Hodgson, G.M., 'The Effects of Joint Production and Fixed Capital in Linear Economic Analysis', mimeo, Manchester 1974.

Holt, D. von, Pasero, U., and Roth, V., *Aspekte der Marxschen Theorie 2. Zur Wertformanalyse*, Frankfurt 1974.

Howitt, P.W., 'Walras and Monetary Theory', *Western Economic Journal*, vol. 11, 1973, pp. 487-99.

Hume, D., 'Of Money', in A.A. Walters, ed., *Money and Banking*, Harmondsworth 1973 (first published 1752).

Jones, R.A., 'The Origin and Development of Media of Exchange', *Journal of Political Economy*, vol. 84, 1976, pp. 757-75.

Kay, G., 'A Note on Abstract Labour', *Bulletin of the Conference of Socialist Economists*, March 1976.

Keynes, J.M., 'A Monetary Theory of Production', in *Der Stand und die nächste Zukunft der Konjunkturforschung. Festschrift für A. Spiethoff*, Berlin 1933, pp. 123-125.

Knight, F.H., *The Ethics of Competition*, New York 1935.

Krause, U., 'Die Logik der Wertform', in *Mehrwert* 13, Berlin 1977.

——, 'Über negative Werte', mimeo, Bremen 1977.

——, 'Elemente einer multisektoralen Analyse der Arbeit', Diskussionsbeiträge zur Politischen Okonomie nr. 5, Bremen 1978.

Kurz, H.D., *Zur neoricardianischen Theorie des Allgemeinen Gleichgewichts der Produktion und Zirkulation*, Berlin 1977.

——, 'Rent Theory in a Multisectoral Model', *Oxford Economic Papers*, vol. 30, 1978, pp. 16-37.

Maarek, G., *Introduction au 'Capital' de Karl Marx. Un Essai de Formalisation*, Paris 1975.

Marx, K., *Capital* Volume 1, Harmondsworth 1976.

——, *Theories of Surplus-Value*, Part 3, London 1972.

Mehrwert 13: 'Beiträge zum Transformationsproblem', Berlin 1977.

Metcalfe, J.S., and Steedman, I., 'Reswitching and Primary Input Use', *Economic Journal*, vol. 82, 1972, pp. 140-157.

Morgenstern, O. and Thompson, G.L., *Mathematical Theory of Expanding and Contracting Economies*, Lexington 1976.

Morishima, M., *Marx's Economics. A Dual Theory of Value and Growth*, Cambridge 1973.

——, *Walras' Economics. A Pure Theory of Capital and Money*, Cambridge 1977.

Morishima, M. and Catephores, G., *Value, Exploitation and Growth. Marx in the Light of Modern Economic Theory*, London 1978.

Nanninga, J., 'Tauschwert und Wert. Eine sprachkritische Rekonstruktion des Fundaments der Politischen Ökonomie', mimeo, Hamburg 1975.

Newman, P., 'Production of Commodities by Means of Commodities', *Schweizerische Zeitschrift für Volkswirtschaft und Statistik*, Bd. 98, 1962, pp. 58-75.

Nikaido, H., *Convex Structures and Economic Theory*, New York 1968.

Nutzinger, H.G., 'Concepts of Value in Linear Economic Models', *Operations Research Verfahren* 26, 1977, pp. 717-724.

Nutzinger, H.G. and Wolfstetter, E., eds., *Die Marxsche Theorie und ihre Kritik. Eine Textsammlung zur Kritik der Politischen Ökonomie*, 2 Bde. Frankfurt 1974.

Ostroy, J.M. and Starr, R.M., 'Money and the Decentralization of Exchange', *Econometrica*, vol. 42, 1974, pp. 1093-1113.

Pashukanis, E., *Law and Marxism*, London 1978 (first published in Russian 1924).

Pasinetti, L.L., *Lectures on the Theory of Production*, London 1977.

Pethig, R., *Zur Theorie der Transaktionen. Ein Beitrag zur mikroökonomischen Grundlegung der Geldtheorie*, Tübingen 1975.

Picard, R., 'Zum quantitativen Wertproblem', in *Gesellschaft*, H.G. Backhaus, ed., Bd. 3, Frankfurt 1975.

Plasmeijer, H.W., 'Marx' anatomie van de burgerlijke maatschappij', mimeo, Groningen 1976.

Projektgruppe Entwicklung des Marxschen Systems, *Das Kapitel vom Geld*, Berlin 1973.

Rancière. J., *Der Begriff der Kritik und die Kritik der Politischen Ökonomie*, Berlin 1972.

Rauner, R.M., *Samuel Bailey and the Classical Theory of Value*, London 1961.

Rehberg, K.S. and Zinn, K.G., 'Die Marxsche Werttheorie als Basistheorie interdependenter Verteilungsstrukturen im Kapitalismus', *Jahrbücher für Nationalökonomie und Statistik*, Bd. 191, 1977, pp. 396-427.

Remak, R., 'Kann die Volkswirtschaftslehre eine exakte Wissenschaft werden?', *Jahrbücher für Nationalökonomie und Statistik*, Bd. 131, 1929, pp. 703-735.

Ricardo, D., *On the Principles of Political Economy and Taxation*, P. Sraffa, ed., Cambridge 1951.

Robinson, J., *Economic Philosophy*, London 1964.

Roncaglia, A., *Sraffa and the Theory of Prices*, New York 1978.

Roth, V., 'Zum wissenschaftlichen Anspruch der Wertform Analyse', mimeo, Konstanz 1976.

Rubin, I.I., *Essays on Marx's Theory of Value*, Detroit 1972.

Sahlins, M., *Stone Age Economics*, London 1974.

Samuelson, P.A., 'What Classical and Neoclassical Monetary Theory Really Was', *Canadian Journal of Economics*, vol. 1, 1968, pp. 1-16.

Schaik, A. van, *Reproduction and Fixed Capital*, Tilburg 1976.

Schefold, B., *Mr Sraffa on Joint Production*, privately published, Basle 1971.

Schlicht, E., *Einführung in die Verteilungstheorie*, Hamburg 1976.

Schumpeter, J.A., *Das Wesen des Geldes*, Göttingen 1970.

Schwartz, J.T., *Lectures on the Mathematical Method in Analytical Economics*, New York 1961.

Schwartz, J., ed., *The Subtle Anatomy of Capitalism*, Santa Monica 1977.

Semmler, W., *Zur Theorie der Reproduktion und Akkumulation*, Berlin 1977.

Sen, A., 'On the Labour Theory of Value: Some Methodological Issues', *Cambridge Journal of Economics*, vol. 2, 1978, pp. 175-190.

Seneta, E., *Non-negative Matrices*, London 1973.

Smith, A., *The Wealth of Nations*, London 1970 (first published 1776).

Sohn-Rethel, A., *Warenform-Denkform*, Frankfurt 1978.

Sraffa, P., *Production of Commodities by Means of Commodities*, with an afterword by B. Schefold, Cambridge 1960.

Steedman, I., *Marx after Sraffa*, London 1977.

Steiger, O., 'Prelude to a Theory of a Monetary Economy. A Note on the Origins of Modern Macroeconomics', in *Diskussionsbeiträge zur Politischen Ökonomie*, Nr. 3, Bremen 1978.

Ulph, A.M. and Ulph, D.T., 'Transaction Costs in General Equilibrium Theory: A Survey', *Economica*, vol. 42, 1975, pp. 355-71.

Visser, H., 'Marx on Money', *Kredit und Kapital*, Bd. 10, 1977, pp. 266-87.

Vogt, W., 'Reine Theorie marktwirtschaftlich-kapitalistischer Systeme', *Diskussionsbeiträge zur Politischen Ökonomie*, Nr. 1, Regensburg 1976.

Walras, L., *Mathematische Theorie der Preisbestimmung der wirtschaftlichen Güter. Vier Denkschriften*, Glashütten 1972 (first published in French, 1876).

Weintraub, E.R., 'The Microfoundations of Macroeconomics: A Critical Survey', *Journal of Economic Literature*, vol. 15, 1977, pp. 1-23.

Weizsäcker, C.C. von, 'Notizen zur Marxschen Wertlehre', in H.G. Nutzinger, E. Wolfstetter, eds., *Die Marxsche Theorie und ihre Kritik II*, Frankfurt 1974, pp. 94-107.

Wicksell, K., *Geldzins und Güterpreise*, Aalen 1968 (first published 1898).

Willett, T.D., 'A Defence of A. Smith's Deer and Beaver Models', *The Journal of Economic Studies*, Bd 3/2, 1968, pp. 29-32.

Williamson, O.E., *Markets and Hierarchies: Analysis and Antitrust Implications*, New York 1975.

Wittmann, W., 'Die extremale Wirtschaft. Robert Remak—ein Vorläufer der Aktivitätsanalyse', *Jahrbücher für Nationalökonomie und Statistik*, Bd. 180, 1967, pp. 397-409.

Wolfstetter, E., *Wert, Profitrate und Beschäftigung. Aspekte* der Marxschen und der klassischen Wirtschaftstheorie, Frankfurt 1977.

Woods, J.E., *Mathematical Economics. Topics in Multi-Sectoral Economics*, London 1978.

Additional Bibliography

Benetti, C., Cartelier, J., *Marchands, salariat et capitalistes*, Paris, 1980.

Bidard, C., 'Travail et salaire chez Sraffa', *Revue économique*, 1981, pp. 448-467.

Bowles, S., and Gintis, H., 'Professor Morishima on Heterogeneous Labour and Marxian Value Theory', *Cambridge Journal of Economics*, 2, 1978, pp. 311-314.

Bowles, S. and Gintis, H., 'Labour Heterogeneity and the Labour Theory of Value: A Reply', *Cambridge Journal of Economics*, 5, 1981 a, pp. 285-288.

Bowles, S. and Gintis, H., 'Structure and Practice in the Labour Theory of Value', *Review of Radical Political Economics*, 12 (4), 1981 b, pp. 1-26.

Catephores, G., 'On Heterogeneous Labour and the Labour Theory of Value', *Cambridge Journal of Economics*, 5, 1981, pp. 273-280.

Cayatte, J.L., 'Méthode de calcul du degré de complexité de la force de travail', *Revue économique*, 1981, p. 563-580.

Chaillou, J., 'L'indétermination possible de la valeur travail et du taux de plus-value', *Revue d'économie politique*, 4, 1980, pp. 481-488.

Eldred, M. and Hanlon, M., 'Reconstructing Value-Form Analysis', mimeo, n.d.

Elson, D., ed., *Value. The Representation of Labour in Capitalism*, London 1979.

Flaschel, P., 'Notes on Sraffa's Standard Commodity and Related Questions', Diskussionspapier Nr. 1, FB 10, Freie Universität, Berlin 1980.

Fujimori, Y., 'The Fundamental Marxian Theorem with Heterogeneous Labour', *Economic Studies Quarterly*, 29, 1978, pp. 282-286.

Fujimori, Y., *Modern Analysis of Value Theory*, University of Josai, 1981.

Ganssmann, H., 'Transformations of Physical Conditions of Production: Steedman's Economic Metaphysics', *Economy and Society*, 10 (4) 1981, pp. 403-422.

Gesellschaft. Beiträge zur Marxschen Theorie Bd. 13 (Kolloquium 'Quantitative Probleme werttheoretischer Argumentationen', Frankfurt 1978, ed. M. Cogoy), Frankfurt 1979.

Hinrichsen, D., Krause, U., 'A Substitution Theorem for Joint Production Models with Disposal Processes', *Operations Research Verfahren*, 41, 1981, pp. 287-291.

Holländer, H., 'A Note on Heterogeneous Labour and Exploitation', *Diskussionsbeiträge zur Politischen Ökonomie* Nr. 14, Dortmund 1978.

Hollard, M. and Tortajada, R., 'Uber das Reduktionsproblem', in P. Thal, ed., *200 Jahre Adam Smith' 'Reichtum der Nationen'*, Glashütten 1976.

Krause, U., 'Abstract Labour in General Joint Systems', mimeo, Bremen 1979.

— —, 'Heterogeneous Labour and the Fundamental Marxian Theorem', *Review of Economic Studies*, 48, 1981 a, pp. 173-178.

— —, 'Marxian Inequalities in a von Neumann Setting', *Zeitschrift für Nationalökonomie*, 41 (1/2), 1981 b, pp. 59-67.

Kurz, H.D., 'Sraffa after Marx (reviewing: Ian Steedman, Marx after Sraffa)', *Australian Economic Papers*, June 1979, pp. 52-70

Leviathan. Zeitschrift für Sozialwissenschaft, (H.G. Haupt *et al.*, eds.), Jahrgang 7, Heft 4, 1979, pp. 537-583.

McKenna, E., 'A Comment on Bowles and Gintis' Marxian Theory of Value', *Cambridge Journal of Economics*, 5, 1981, pp. 281-284.

Morishima, M., 'S. Bowles and H. Gintis on the Marxian Theory of Value and Heterogeneous Labour', *Cambridge Journal of Economics*, 2, 1978, pp. 305-309.

Reich, U.P., 'From Heterogeneous to Abstract Labour and the Definition of Segmentation', *Acta Oeconomica*, 23 (3/4), 1979, pp. 339-351.

Roemer, J.E., *Analytical Foundation of Marxian Economic Theory*, Cambridge, 1981.

Schneider, J., *Der Beitrag der Arbeitswertlehre zur Theorie der kapitalistischen Warenproduktion*, Frankfurt 1980.

Steedman, I., 'Heterogeneous Labour and "Classical" Theory', Metroeconomica, 32 (1), 1980, pp. 39-50.

Steenge, A.E., *Stability and Standard Commodities in Multi-sector Input-Output Models*, Groningen 1980.

Teplitz-Sembitzky, W., 'Werte, Preise und Gleichgewicht—Ein Beitrag zum Transformationsproblem', *Jahrbücher für Nationalökonomie und Statistik*, Bd. 192, 1978, pp. 493-513.